MASTERING
CAPITAL RAISING

REBECCA MEIJLINK

Legal Notice
This book is copyright-protected. This book is only for personal use. You cannot amend, distribute, sell, use, quote, or paraphrase any part of the content within this book without the publisher's consent. The contents of this book may not be reproduced, duplicated, or transmitted in any form or by any means, electronic or mechanical, including photocopying, recording, or any information storage and retrieval system, without the explicit written permission of the publisher and the author.

Disclaimer Notice
The information in this book is not intended to give any legal, investment, financial, or tax advice. The laws and regulations governing various topics can change rapidly, and the information in this book may need to be updated. You should consult an attorney or other qualified advisor before deciding your legal situation. The advice contained herein may not be suitable for your situation. While the publisher and author have used their best efforts in preparing this book, they make no representations or warranties concerning the accuracy or completeness of the book's contents and expressly disclaim any implied warranties.

ISBN: 978-1-7395640-5-6 (Paperback)
ISBN: 978-1-7395640-6-3 (E-book)
First edition 1.0 (11 November 2023), Updated 9 January 2024
Publisher: AlphaBet Select Ltd, London, United Kingdom

All inquiries should be addressed to the publisher, AlphaBet Select Ltd, London, United Kingdom. The publisher would appreciate being notified of any corrections that should be incorporated in future reprints or subsequent editions of the book. For our contact details, visit our website at **www.alphabetselect.com**.

AlphaBet Select Ltd

Contents

Introduction

With two decades of experience as a Placement Agent, I have authored *"Mastering Capital Raising,"* a comprehensive guide for companies seeking institutional investment. It provides practical insights and strategies for navigating the complex capital raising landscape, from crafting a compelling pitch to closing the deal.

I wrote briefing notes for my clients as a checklist before embarking on an equity raise. In this book, I am making the contents available to a broader audience, geared towards Boards, Founders, and CEOs new to institutional capital raising.

Many companies have unrealistic expectations about timelines and mistakenly believe that the storytelling techniques that work with high net-worth investors will translate to success with institutional investors. However, institutional capital raising is a distinct ballgame with its own rules, akin to a demanding 18-hole golf course rather than a leisurely 9-hole round.

"Mastering Capital Raising" delves into critical aspects such as readiness for a capital raise, creating an impressive pitch deck, preparing an electronic data room, determining the valuation, and handling frequently asked questions. If you fail to prepare, you prepare to fail. The book emphasises global considerations such as ESG factors, UN Sustainable Development Goals, diversity, and inclusion. Additionally, it explores navigating regulatory constraints, compliance, and considerations for marketing materials and investor interactions.

Engaging with investors and building relationships is paramount to capital raising. The book explores success metrics, investor identification, segmentation, and pitching strategies. It highlights the importance of thorough due diligence on investors and delves into the dynamics and execution of successful investor meetings and post-meeting excellence. It also provides insights into investor processes, including decision-making, due diligence, investment committees, and on-site visits.

"Mastering Capital Raising" empowers you to become an institutional capital raising expert, fostering confidence in your ability to succeed in this ever-evolving ecosystem. It emphasises the attainability of authority, mastery, and consistent growth. Sealing the deal requires a sharp focus on negotiation tactics, legal documentation, and anticipating potential investor concerns.

The book underscores the importance of continuous investor relations and formulating the equity story with clear exit strategies in mind.

It also explores future capital raising prospects, including modern methodologies like crowdfunding, social media strategies, and blockchain technology. It contemplates the innovative analytical, emotional, and predictive power of AI-driven capital raising robots and touches on cybersecurity risks.

Chapter 1 The Importance of Capital Raising

1.1 Why Raise Capital

CEOs might raise capital to fund growth, mergers and acquisitions, expand into new markets, or develop new products or services. There are pros and cons of raising capital from external investors and the different types of capital available. Carefully weigh the pros and cons of raising capital before deciding which route to take.

Reasons why CEOs choose to raise capital

If a private company wants to grow their business quickly, it may need to raise capital to finance that growth. This could include hiring new employees, expanding into new markets, or developing new products or services. Sometimes, CEOs may see new opportunities for their business that require additional capital to invest in. For example, they may see a chance to expand into a new market or acquire a competitor. Undercapitalised companies often have difficulty investing in new products, services, and markets. This can limit their growth potential and make them less competitive.

Without enough capital, a business may be unable to pay its bills, such as rent, salaries, and inventory costs. This can lead to many problems, including late payments, service interruptions, and bankruptcy. If a business does not have enough cash reserves, it may be forced to close its doors if faced with a financial setback.

A business with a positive cash flow is more likely to be successful. Raising capital can help to improve a business's cash flow by providing the funds needed to cover operating expenses and invest in growth opportunities. Businesses can better weather economic downturns or unexpected challenges by having a financial cushion.

How to mitigate the risks associated with undercapitalisation

- *Maintain a healthy debt-to-equity ratio:* A debt-to-equity ratio is a financial measure that compares a company's total debt to its total equity. A high debt-to-equity ratio indicates that a company relies heavily on debt to finance its operations. This makes a company more vulnerable to financial problems if interest rates rise or the company experiences a decline in revenue.
- *Carefully manage cash flow:* Manage cash flow carefully. This means tracking income and expenses closely, forecasting future cash needs, and developing a budget to ensure enough cash to cover all obligations.
- *Develop a contingency plan:* Businesses should develop a contingency plan if they experience a financial setback or the capital raising window closes due to a downturn in the economy or a collapse of the markets. This plan should outline the business's steps to reduce costs, increase revenue, or raise additional capital.
- *Diversify funding sources:* Businesses should diversify to reduce reliance on any source. This could include using a combination of debt, equity, and government grants.

In addition to the above, businesses can use several specific strategies to mitigate the risks associated with undercapitalisation depending on their industry and particular circumstances.

A business in a cyclical industry may want to build up cash reserves during good times to help cushion the blow during downtime. Cyclical industries are sectors of the economy that are sensitive to economic cycles, which means their performance tends to rise and fall with changes in the overall economy. These industries experience periods of expansion and growth during economic upturns (bull markets) and periods of contraction and decline during economic downturns (bear markets). The performance of cyclical industries is closely tied to factors like consumer and business spending, interest rates, and overall economic conditions. Cyclical industries include the consumer discretionary, automotive, manufacturing, construction, financial and commodity industries. While technology is generally seen as a growth sector, it can still be cyclical because demand for technology products and services can fluctuate with economic conditions and business investment.

Some companies finance their operations through internally generated cash flow without relying on external financing. A rapidly expanding business may need additional capital to finance its growth.

In my experience, many companies leave capital raising too late due to unrealistic expectations of their business and the time it takes to raise capital.

Potential downsides to raising equity

- *Dilution of ownership and financial upside*: When raising capital, the company typically gives up some ownership of the company to new investors. This reduces the CEO's potential financial upside. The rationale behind accepting dilution is that the capital raised will significantly grow the company's value, making each share more valuable even though it represents a smaller percentage of the company. Essentially, owning a smaller percentage of a more valuable company can be worth more than owning a larger percentage of a less valuable company.

- *Pressure to perform:* Investors expect to make a return on their investment. *Pressure to perform:* Investors expect to make a return on their investment. This pressure can sometimes lead to stress and the temptation to make short-term decisions prioritising immediate gains over long-term sustainability and growth.
- *More scrutiny and reporting requirements:* With outside investors comes increased scrutiny and reporting requirements. The CEO must provide investors with updates, financial statements, and other information. This can be very time-consuming and distract from the day-to-day running of the business.
- *Loss of privacy:* With external investors involved, sensitive information about the company's operations or financials may need to be shared. This could compromise confidentiality or trade secrets.
- *Loss of control:* Investors may also have a say in business operations. If an investor takes a majority stake, this could mean the CEO has less control over the company's strategic direction and day-to-day operations.

These considerations underscore the importance of a balanced approach to raising equity, ensuring that the benefits outweigh the potential downsides and align with the company's long-term goals.

The degree of control loss depends significantly on the negotiation power of the original owners during the investment process. Stronger negotiation can lead to retaining more control. The consequences of giving up control should be properly understood.

Potential negative consequences of loss of control

When a CEO loses control of their company to investors, it can significantly impact its operations, culture, and long-term direction.

- *Loss of Vision and Direction:* As the founder or visionary, the CEO often has a clear vision for the company's future. When investors take control, they may have different priorities and goals, which can lead to a disconnect between the company's leadership and its employees. This can result in a lack of focus and direction, making it difficult for the company to achieve its long-term objectives.
- *Short-Term Focus:* Investors often focus on short-term gains, such as increasing profits or maximising shareholder value. This can pressure the company to prioritise immediate financial returns over long-term growth and sustainability. This short-term focus can damage the company's reputation, relationships with customers and partners, and overall competitive advantage.
- *Risk of Being Ousted:* In extreme cases, if most investors or the majority shareholder are dissatisfied with the CEO's performance or direction, the investor might push for a change in leadership. This can lead to the founder or CEO being fired or replaced.
- *Reduced Employee Morale and Engagement:* When employees feel that the company's leadership is not aligned

with their values or interests, it can lead to a decline in morale and engagement. This can result in decreased productivity, increased absenteeism, and a higher turnover rate. A disengaged workforce can significantly hinder the company's ability to achieve its goals.

- *Cultural Changes:* Investors may introduce new policies, procedures, or management styles that are not aligned with the company's existing culture. This can lead to cultural clashes and a loss of the company's unique identity. A change in company culture can alienate employees and make it challenging to attract and retain top talent.

- *Negative Impact on Customer Relationships:* A shift in company direction or values can affect customer relationships, particularly if these changes lead to alterations in product quality, customer service, or company ethos.

- *Power Struggles and Conflicts:* When there is a power shift, it can create uncertainty and instability within the company. This can lead to power struggles between factions, such as the original leadership team and the new investor-backed management. These conflicts can divert time and resources from the company's core business operations.

- *Loss of Innovation and Risk-Taking*: Investors may be more risk-averse than the original leadership, leading to decreased innovation and a reluctance to pursue new opportunities. This can stifle the company's growth and make it less competitive in the long run.

I have seen all the above scenarios play out in practice. Understanding the downside is essential. Money comes with strings attached. You must carefully weigh the pros and cons of raising capital before deciding.

If a company decides that raising capital is a necessity for their business, they must ensure they partner with the right investor who shares their vision, or else there may be trouble down the line. If you are onboarding more than one investor, they, too, need to be aligned.

1.2 Capital Structure

The capital structure of a private company is the mix of debt and equity that the company uses to finance its operations. Debt is money the company borrows from lenders, such as banks or investment firms. Equity is ownership in the company, which equity investors typically provide.

The optimal capital structure for a private company will vary depending on several factors, including the company's stage of growth, its industry, and its financial condition. For example, early-stage companies may rely more on equity financing as they may not qualify for traditional debt financing because of their lack of track record and financial history. More mature companies can use a mix of debt and equity financing to finance their growth.

Although this book is focused on raising equity, I will also give you an overview of other types of funding available.

Main different types of debt financing and equity investors

Debt financing

When interest rates are low, taking on debt can offer a cost-effective way to access liquidity. A company can benefit from the difference between the investment returns and the cost of servicing the debt provided it is confident the expected returns from the business activities will exceed the interest payments on the debt. It may also be a good time to consider refinancing existing loans. By refinancing at a lower interest rate, the company can potentially lower its monthly payments and save money over the long term.

Secured debt generally attracts a lower interest rate compared to unsecured debt. Secured debt is backed by collateral, such as property or assets, which gives the lender some assurance in case of default. The collateral reduces the risk for the lender, allowing them to charge a lower interest rate.

Unsecured debt has no collateral attached to it, and the interest rate will depend on factors such as the borrower's credit history and financial stability. Lenders may offer more favourable interest rates to borrowers with good credit scores since they are perceived as less risky.

Evaluate your options and consider factors such as interest rates, repayment terms, and your ability to fulfil your financial obligations before making any decisions regarding debt raising. Choosing the most suitable form of debt financing depends on a company's financial situation, growth plans, and risk appetite.

Classic examples of debt financing

Government loans: Government loans can be a good option for companies with difficulty qualifying for traditional bank loans. These loans offer more favourable terms, such as lower interest rates and flexible repayment options, and are designed to support broader economic objectives. Obtaining a government loan can involve a complex and time-consuming application process. Businesses should be prepared for detailed paperwork and potentially lengthy processing times.

Bank loans: Bank loans are a common form of debt financing for private companies. Banks typically offer a variety of loan products, such as term loans, revolving lines of credit, and invoice financing.

- *Term loans* provide a lump sum of capital for a specific purpose, such as expanding operations, acquiring assets, or launching new products. They come with fixed repayment schedules and interest rates, allowing businesses to plan their finances efficiently.
- *Revolving lines of credit* provide businesses with a flexible source of financing. Companies can draw funds as needed, up to a predefined credit limit. This type of loan is particularly valuable for managing working capital fluctuations and addressing short-term liquidity needs.
- *Invoice financing,* also known as accounts receivable financing, enables companies to unlock the value of their outstanding invoices. Banks advance a percentage of the invoice amount, allowing businesses to access cash flow without waiting for customers to settle their invoices.

Corporate bonds: Corporate bonds are securities companies issue to raise money from investors. These bonds represent a contractual agreement between the issuing company and the bondholder, with the company promising to pay periodic interest (coupon payments) and return the principal amount at maturity. Corporate bonds offer specified maturity dates ranging from years to decades. Credit ratings assess issuer creditworthiness, influencing risk perception. Bonds can be traded in the secondary market.

Venture debt: Venture debt is a type of financing for early-stage companies. Venture debt providers typically offer higher-risk, higher-reward loans than traditional banks. This type of financing can boost early-stage companies without diluting ownership or control. This debt can be used for various purposes, including equipment purchases, marketing, and research and development. While venture debt providers are more lenient regarding collateral, they charge higher interest rates and fees. Repayment terms are typically structured with flexible options.

Corporate venture debt: Some larger corporations can finance startups through their venture arms.

Private credit funds: Private credit funds are investment vehicles that pool capital from institutional and high-net-worth investors to invest in non-traded debt securities, such as loans, bonds, and other forms of credit. These funds typically offer investors the potential for higher interest rates compared to traditional banks, making them an attractive option for those seeking better returns. Private credit funds often provide greater flexibility in structuring deals, allowing customised lending terms. This flexibility can make them valuable for borrowers and investors looking for tailored debt solutions outside traditional banking channels.

Other avenues for debt financing

Traditional methods of raising debt financing can be time-consuming, expensive, and difficult to qualify for. As a result, businesses are increasingly exploring innovative methods of raising debt financing that offer more flexibility, lower costs, or faster access to capital.

- *Peer-to-peer lending:* Platforms allow individuals to lend money to others or businesses. This type of financing can be a good option for companies that may not have access to traditional bank loans.

- *Crowdfunding Debt with Tokenisation:* Crowdfunding platforms can be used for equity financing and debt. Businesses can raise small amounts from a large pool of individuals or institutions, creating a diverse pool of lenders. The tokenisation of debt allows businesses to issue digital tokens representing debt instruments. These tokens can be traded on blockchain platforms, providing liquidity and efficiency in debt markets.

- *Social and Green Bonds:* Social and green bonds are specialised debt instruments designed to finance projects with positive social or environmental outcomes. They are part of the broader concept of impact investing, which seeks to generate financial returns alongside social and environmental benefits.

- *Financing through Asset-Backed Securities:* Securitising equipment leases or loans into asset-backed securities can be innovative in raising debt financing, especially for businesses with valuable equipment.

- *Online Invoice Trading:* Online platforms allow businesses to sell their outstanding invoices to investors at a discount, providing immediate cash flow. This is especially beneficial for companies with significant accounts receivable.

- *Revenue-Based Financing (RBF):* In RBF, businesses repay lenders a percentage of their revenue until a predetermined amount is repaid, with no fixed repayment term. This aligns the interests of the lender with the success of the business.

- *Cryptocurrency and Blockchain-Based Financing:* Cryptocurrencies and blockchain technology have enabled new forms of debt financing. Smart contracts on blockchain platforms can automate and secure debt agreements, reducing transaction costs and increasing transparency.

- *Online Supply Chain Financing*: Online supply chain financing platforms allow businesses to access funds based on outstanding invoices. This can help businesses with limited access to traditional financing improve their cash flow and manage their supply chains more effectively.
- *Insurance-Linked Securities (ILS)*: ILS involve raising capital from the capital markets by issuing bonds linked to insurance risks. Insurance companies often use this innovative method to manage risk.

Equity investors

Equity financing is a method of raising capital by selling a portion of the ownership of a company in exchange for cash. This can be achieved through various agreements, including preferred equity, which may have certain conditions attached. These conditions can vary and may include preferences in terms of dividends or liquidation proceeds, as well as other rights that provide additional protection or benefits to the preferred shareholders.

Unlike debt raising, equity financing does not require interest repayments. The company's potential upside will need to be shared with the investor. As the company grows and becomes more successful, the investor will typically benefit from the increase in value and potentially receive dividends or capital gains.

By offering equity to investors, companies can access funds without taking on additional debt or making regular interest payments. This can be particularly advantageous for startups or businesses with limited cash flow, as it allows them to secure funds for growth and expansion while sharing the financial risks and rewards with investors.

Equity financing may involve giving up a certain degree of control and ownership in the company. Founders and existing shareholders may need to consider this trade-off when pursuing equity financing as a funding option. Overall, equity financing can be an effective way for companies to raise capital and fuel their growth while allowing investors to participate in the company's success.

Examples of equity investors

- *Bootstrapping:* Bootstrapping is financing a company's growth using its internal resources, such as revenue and profits. This is usually the case at the idea stage.
- *Family and Friends:* In the early stages, entrepreneurs often raise initial capital from family members and friends who believe in their business idea.
- *Angel investors:* Angel investors are individuals who invest their own money in early-stage companies. Angel investors typically invest smaller amounts of money than venture capitalists. They can provide valuable guidance and mentorship to entrepreneurs. Angel investors play a crucial role in the entrepreneurial ecosystem, bridging the gap between early-stage startups and traditional venture capital firms.
- *HNW Seed Investors:* A seed investor is an individual or group that invests in the early stages of a startup company. Seed investors typically invest between $50,000 and $1 million in exchange for a small equity stake in the company. Seed funding is often used to help startups develop prototypes, conduct market research, and hire key employees. Seed investors are typically wealthy individuals with a strong business success track record. They are often interested in investing in early-stage companies because

they believe that these companies have the potential to grow into large, successful businesses. Seed investors also play a valuable role in providing startups with advice and mentorship.

- *Crowdfunding:* Some platforms allow businesses to raise equity financing from a broad base of investors.
- *Venture capitalists:* Venture capitalists are investment firms that invest in early-stage and growth-stage companies. Venture capitalists typically invest larger amounts of money than angel investors, and they can provide valuable resources and support to entrepreneurs.
- *Strategic Investors:* Companies may invest due to their strategic interest in products, services, or technologies.
- *Private equity:* Private equity firms are investment firms that invest in private companies. Private equity firms typically invest in more mature companies than venture capitalists and may use leverage to finance their investments.
- *Other sources may include* Hedge Funds, Pension Funds, Insurance Companies, and Family Offices.

A hybrid of debt and equity

A convertible note begins as short-term debt and is later converted into equity. Essentially, investors lend money to a company and are repaid with equity instead of principal and interest. It provides flexibility for both the company and investors. Initially, it functions as a short-term debt, allowing investors to provide capital to a company through a loan. However, at a later stage, the convertible note can be converted into equity, meaning that instead of receiving the initial investment back with interest, investors can become shareholders in the company. This hybrid structure allows companies to secure funding while offering potential upside for investors through an equity stake.

Mezzanine financing is a hybrid of debt and equity financing. It includes subordinated debt and other financial instruments that often come with higher interest rates and can convert into equity if specific conditions are met.

Impact of options

The impact of options on a company's capital structure is an important consideration. When executives or employees are granted stock options as part of their compensation packages, it can dilute the ownership stakes of existing shareholders when those options are exercised. This means that the overall distribution of equity within the company may be altered.

Options give the holder the right, but not the obligation, to buy or sell an underlying asset at a predetermined price within a specific time frame. This flexibility can lead to changes in ownership and subsequently affect a company's capital structure. When stock options are exercised, new shares may be issued, increasing the total number of outstanding shares in circulation. Existing shareholders' ownership percentages can decrease proportionally as these new shares enter the market.

This potential dilution effect caused by option exercises has implications for existing shareholders and potential investors. Existing shareholders may see their relative ownership reduced, which could impact voting rights and influence over key decision-making processes within the company. When evaluating its value and investment potential, potential investors analysing a company's capital structure may consider any outstanding stock options.

It is worth noting that while options have implications for the capital structure, they also serve as incentives for executives and employees to drive performance and align their interests with those of shareholders. Options can motivate individuals to work towards increasing shareholder value since they often gain financially through exercising these options when share prices rise. Employees may accept a lower salary with options, appealing to startups or growth-stage companies where cash flow may be limited but growth prospects are high.

1.3 Conflicts between Debt and Equity Investors

Debt and equity investors have different risk profiles and objectives, which can lead to conflicts of interest.

Debt investors are considered senior creditors, meaning they have priority over equity investors in the event of a liquidation. This means that debt investors are less exposed to the risk of losing their investment but have a lower potential return. Equity investors, on the other hand, have a higher potential return, but they also bear more risk. This difference in risk preferences can lead to conflict, as debt investors may pressure the company to take on less risky projects, and equity investors may favour higher-risk projects with the potential for higher returns.

Debt investors typically receive a fixed return through interest payments. Equity investors, on the other hand, receive an uncertain return in the form of dividends or capital gains. This difference in return expectations can lead to conflict, as debt investors may favour policies that increase the company's ability to pay interest. In contrast, equity investors may favour policies that increase the company's stock price.

Debt investors have limited control over the company's operations. Equity investors, on the other hand, have voting rights and can influence the company's decisions through shareholder meetings and proxy voting. This difference in control can lead to conflict, as debt investors may feel that they are not adequately represented in the company's decision-making process.

If the company changes its strategic direction, it may create conflicts with debt investors if the new strategy is perceived as riskier or less likely to generate cash flow.

Economic downturns can lead to increased risk aversion among debt investors, making it more difficult for the company to raise new debt or renegotiate existing debt terms.

Companies should maintain open and transparent communication with debt and equity investors. This will help to build trust and understanding between the two groups and make it easier to resolve conflicts. They should have clear governance structures that define the roles and responsibilities of debt and equity investors. This will help to prevent misunderstandings and ensure that the interests of all investors are considered.

Companies should also closely monitor their financial condition and communicate regularly with investors about any changes that could affect their investments. This will help to prevent surprises and allow investors to take action to protect their investments if necessary.

1.4 Primary versus Secondary Capital Raise

Primary and secondary capital raises refer to different stages and methods of capital acquisition, each with its purposes and implications.

Primary capital raises involve the issuance of new securities (e.g., stocks or bonds) directly by the company to raise capital for its operations, expansion, or other corporate purposes. In the context of equity financing, primary capital raises typically involve the sale of new shares of stock to investors. The primary purpose of a primary capital raise is to raise fresh capital for the company to support its growth, research and development, working capital, acquisitions, or any other business-related activities. The company raises capital from existing and new investors. In primary capital raises, the company's ownership is diluted because new shares or securities are issued to investors. Existing shareholders may see their ownership percentages decrease unless they participate in the capital raise.

A secondary capital raise involves the sale of existing securities (shares of stock) from one of the existing investors or a group of existing investors to another existing or new incoming investor without the company's direct involvement. The primary purpose of a secondary capital raise is to allow existing shareholders to monetise their investments by selling their shares to other investors. It gives them an exit. This process does not provide new capital to the company.

An incoming investor may want to buy the shares of the initial early-stage investors, which often will be made up of many high-net-worth investors. It simplifies communication and leads to more efficient decision-making processes. In secondary capital raises, the company's ownership remains unchanged because the company doesn't issue new shares. Ownership changes hands among existing shareholders and new investors.

Directors and officers of the company owe fiduciary duties to shareholders. They must act in the best interests of the company and its shareholders, which can lead to legal complications if conflicts of interest or breaches of duty are alleged. Navigating the legal complexities of secondary transactions requires careful planning, legal counsel, and a thorough understanding of the applicable laws and regulations.

Consulting with experienced legal professionals who specialise in securities law is highly advisable to ensure compliance and minimise legal risks. Other remaining existing shareholders may have contractual rights that need to be considered in a secondary transaction. These rights could include the right of first refusal, tag-along rights, or drag-along rights, which may require the company or existing shareholders to offer the securities to other parties before completing the transaction.

By understanding whether a secondary sale involves founder shares or management selling, incoming investors can gain valuable insights into how committed and confident the founders and management team are about their company's future trajectory. Investors want assurance that founders are not simply looking for an exit strategy by selling their existing shares (secondary capital raise).

1.5 Stages in the Company's Life Cycle

Idea or Seed Stage - The idea or seed stage marks the beginning of a company's journey, where entrepreneurs and innovators develop their initial ideas into potential business concepts. During this stage, individuals brainstorm and research to validate their ideas, exploring market opportunities and probable customer demand.

R&D Stage - The research and development (R&D) stage is where companies focus on refining their ideas and turning them into tangible products or services. This stage involves conducting in-depth research, prototyping, and testing to ensure that the product or service meets the desired standards and addresses customers' needs.

The Commercialization and Product Launch Stage - Once a product or service has been developed, the commercialisation stage comes into play. Companies in this stage focus on creating marketing strategies to introduce their offerings to the target market. They develop pricing strategies, establish distribution channels, and create promotional campaigns to generate awareness and drive sales.

The Growth Stage - In the growth stage, companies experience rapid expansion and increased market share. They have established a solid customer base and are focused on scaling their operations. Companies in this stage often invest in expanding their workforce, enhancing production capabilities, and entering new markets to capitalise on their success.

The Acquisition Stage - During the acquisition stage, companies acquire other businesses to expand their market presence or access new technologies or resources. This stage allows companies to consolidate their position within the industry and further strengthen their competitive advantage.

Global Expansion - Global expansion can be a significant milestone depending on the company's industry and goals. This could be relevant in the Growth or Acquisition Stages as companies seek to enter international markets.

Strategic Partnerships and Alliances - Throughout various stages, companies may form strategic partnerships or alliances with other organisations to access resources, technology, or distribution channels.

Maturity Stage - After the Growth Stage, many companies reach a point of maturity where they may experience slower growth but continue to generate stable revenues. This stage often requires a focus on operational efficiency and customer retention.

Decline Stage - In some cases, companies may enter a Decline Stage, facing challenges such as declining market demand, outdated products, or increased competition. Managing decline can involve restructuring, divestitures, or exiting certain markets.

The Pre-IPO Stage - The pre-IPO (Initial Public Offering) stage occurs when a company prepares to go public by offering its shares for sale to the general public. In this stage, companies typically engage in financial audits, regulatory compliance assessments, valuation analysis, and drafting prospectuses. Preparing for an IPO involves extensive planning and coordination with investment banks and legal advisors to ensure a successful transition into a publicly traded company.

Post-IPO Stage - After a successful IPO, companies enter the post-IPO stage, becoming publicly traded entities. This stage involves ongoing regulatory compliance, financial reporting, and efforts to maintain and grow the company's stock price.

Exit Strategies - Not all companies go public; some may pursue alternative exit strategies like mergers and acquisitions (M&A) or management buyouts.

1.6 Capital Raising Routes

There are several different ways for private companies to raise money. The best route for a private company to raise money will vary depending on circumstances. There are factors that companies should consider when choosing a capital raising method: their growth stage, industry, financial condition, and management team.

Early-stage companies may consider bootstrapping or raising money from friends and family. More mature companies will consider raising money from angel investors, venture capitalists, or private equity firms.

Some industries, such as technology and healthcare, are more attractive to investors than others. This means that companies in these industries may have easier access to capital.

Companies with strong financial statements will attract more institutional investors than those with weak ones.

Adapting from HNWI to institutional requirements

Transitioning from raising capital from friends, family and high net worth individuals (HNWI) to institutional investors can be challenging for many CEOs. While they may have successfully told compelling stories and attracted investment from HNWI, securing funding from institutions requires a more process-driven approach. CEOs sometimes assume that what worked in the past will also work with institutional investors.

They often find themselves frustrated by the thorough questioning and due diligence processes institutions undertake before making investment decisions. This can lead to impatience and unease during the fundraising process. They fail to recognise the importance of documentation.

CEOs must recognise that institutional investors have unique requirements and considerations compared to individual investors. What worked in the past may no longer work. Institutions typically have more resources, expertise, and risk management processes when evaluating potential investments.

Before committing funds, they want to thoroughly understand the business model, financials, market dynamics, competitive landscape, and growth prospects. Instead of becoming disheartened or impatient with the process, CEOs should focus on adapting their approach to meet institutional investor expectations. This may involve presenting comprehensive business plans supported by robust financial projections, providing detailed market research and analysis, showcasing a strong management team with relevant experience, addressing potential risks proactively through effective risk mitigation strategies, and demonstrating scalability potential.

Furthermore, building relationships with institutional investors takes time; it is not solely about quick wins like it might be with HNWI. Cultivating trust through transparent communication channels is essential throughout the entire funding journey. In summary, transitioning from raising capital from HNWI to institutions requires understanding their needs and expectations. Patience is key as CEOs navigate through meticulous due diligence processes while adapting their storytelling approach accordingly. Align your strategy with institution-specific requirements and cultivate strong relationships over time.

1.7 Series A-D Terminology

In the world of equity financing, the terms "Series Seed", "Series A," "Series B," "Series C," "Series D," and "Pre-IPO" refer to different stages of raising equity capital. These stages reflect the growth and maturity of a company, and each round has its specific characteristics and purposes.

Series Seed is raised from angels and early-stage VCs to refine the core product and market. Amounts raised may vary from $250k to $2 million.

Series A is often the first significant round of business funding to scale the product, expand the user base and refine the business model. Startups that have developed a track record (an established user base, consistent revenue figures, or some other key performance indicator) use Series A funding to optimise their product or service further. This round typically involves venture capital firms, though angel investors may also participate. Series A rounds can range from $2 million to $15 million or more, depending on the industry and the company's valuation.

Series B is about taking businesses to the next level, past the development stage. Companies that have gone through the Series A phase have developed a substantial user base and have proven to investors that they are prepared for success on a larger scale. This round usually sees a mix of venture capitalists and possibly new investors, including more strategic players who can offer partnerships alongside funding. The amounts can vary significantly but are generally larger than Series A, often in the tens of millions of dollars.

Companies that make it to Series C funding rounds are already quite successful. These companies seek more funding to help them develop new products, expand into new markets, or even acquire other companies. Series C investors often include hedge funds, investment banks, private equity firms, and large secondary market groups. Series C funding can range significantly, often reaching hundreds of millions.

Not all companies go through a Series D round. When they do, it could be for reasons like targeting new markets, making acquisitions, or because they need more time before going public. This round can include a mix of previous and new investors, often those looking for a shorter-term opportunity before an anticipated IPO. The amounts can be quite variable and large, depending on the company's valuation and strategy.

Pre-IPO is the funding stage before a company goes public. The goal here is often to adjust the company's valuation in preparation for the IPO. Pre-IPO investors are typically late-stage venture capitalists, private equity firms, hedge funds, and sometimes large individual investors looking for one last opportunity to invest before the company goes public. The amount raised during this stage depends heavily on the anticipated valuation of the company at the time of the IPO.

Each round of funding is critical in its own way and marks a significant milestone in a company's journey towards growth and market dominance. The terms of investment, valuation, and the amount of capital raised can vary widely based on the industry, market conditions, and the specific growth plans of the company.

1.8 Competition

The competition is invisible. You do not see who you compete with; many conversations are one-on-one meetings. There is a lot of competition, and you must be at the top of your game to succeed. Going to conferences gives you more insight into the landscape. Competition in raising capital from investors varies across the stages of a company's life cycle.

Early Stage (Seed and Series A)
- *Competition:* Many startups are typically competing for funding at this stage. Many of these companies are in the idea or prototype phase, and the market is often saturated with similar ideas or products.

- *Investor Availability:* Early-stage investors, such as angel investors and venture capital firms specialising in early-stage investments, are abundant but selective. They are willing to take higher risks for potentially higher returns. However, the amount of capital they provide is usually smaller compared to later stages.
- *Pitching Dynamics:* Given the high risk and potential lack of a proven track record, startups need a compelling pitch and a clear vision to stand out.

Mid Stage (Series B and C)

- *Competition:* The competition among companies at this stage is often less intense than in the early stages. Many startups fail to reach this point, leading to a natural filtering process.
- *Investor Availability:* The number of investors specialising in mid-stage funding is lower compared to early-stage investors. However, these investors typically provide larger sums of money and are more focused on scaling and growing the company.
- *Pitching Dynamics:* Companies at this stage must demonstrate strong growth potential, a scalable business model, and a clear path to profitability to attract investors.

Late Stage (Series D and Beyond) and IPO

- *Competition:* There's generally less competition because few companies make it this far. Those that do are usually well-established with a proven track record.
- *Investor Availability:* Although there are fewer late-stage and public market investors, they can invest large amounts of capital. These investors are typically more risk-averse and look for companies with stable revenues and clear market dominance.

- *Pitching Dynamics:* Companies at this stage must showcase financial stability, market leadership, and a strong executive team. They often attract different types of investors, such as hedge funds, private equity firms, and the general public (in the case of an IPO).

Overall, while more companies may pitch in the early stages, the competition remains high across all stages due to different factors. The availability of investors varies, with more early-stage investors willing to take higher risks for smaller stakes and fewer late-stage investors who provide larger amounts of capital for lower risks.

1.9 Common Misconceptions

Many misconceptions about capital raising can lead entrepreneurs to make mistakes or miss out on opportunities. Here are some of the most common misconceptions.

Venture capital is the only source of capital for startups: Venture capital (VC) is private equity funding typically provided to early-stage companies with high growth potential. VC is not the only source of capital available to startups. Many other types of investors exist, such as angel investors, crowdfunding platforms, and government grants.

You need to be in Silicon Valley to raise money: While Silicon Valley is a major hub for venture capital, there are many investors located outside of Silicon Valley. Companies can reach out to investors all over the world.

It is easy to raise money if you have a great idea: Many entrepreneurs believe that investors will be lining up to give them money if they have a great idea. However, this is not always the case. Investors also seek a strong team, a viable business model, and a large addressable market. It takes much more than just a great idea.

It does not take much time to raise money: It depends, but generally, it takes longer than expected. The amount of time it takes to raise money can vary depending on the stage of the company, the industry, and the prevailing market conditions. Be realistic about the time commitment involved. Raising money can be time-consuming. Many companies leave it too late and then run out of money. In a bull market, you can budget for the raise to take a year. In. a bear market, it may take two years.

You only need to raise money once: Many entrepreneurs believe they will be set for life once they raise funding. However, this is not always the case. As businesses grow, they often need to raise additional funding rounds to support their growth. You may raise capital from one large investor, so you never need to go out to the market again. Usually, capital raising is an ongoing process. You should prepare the next as soon as you close one round.

You need a perfect pitch deck to raise money: A pitch deck is a presentation that entrepreneurs use to introduce their business to investors. While a good pitch deck is important, there are other things investors look at. They will also want to see a solid business plan, financial projections, and evidence of market traction. A good deck is merely the starting point.

Investors only want to invest in high-tech companies: While many focus on high-tech companies, others are interested in investing in various industries. Entrepreneurs should do their research to identify investors who are a good fit for their business and sector focus.

You need to have a lot of connections to raise money: While connections can be helpful, having connections is unnecessary. Many investors are willing to invest in new companies without any prior connections. You must understand the difference between investors properly to pitch to them accordingly.

1.10 What are the Pain Points

Your capital raising pitch needs to be clear, concise, and persuasive. It should clearly articulate your company's value proposition, target market, and financial projections. It is not a one-off exercise. You will continuously improve the story as you receive constructive feedback from investors.

It can be difficult, and expensive to identify potential investors who are interested in your company.

Private companies may not have the same visibility and credibility as public companies. This can make it more challenging to attract investors.

Once you have identified potential investors, you must build relationships with them. This can take time and effort, especially if the investor is not based in your home country. When an investor expresses interest in investing in your company, you must undergo due diligence. This can also be a time-consuming and complex process and can take many months.

No deal is done until the money is in the bank. Once you have completed the due diligence process and reached an agreement with an investor, you must close the deal. This involves negotiating the final terms of the investment and signing the necessary paperwork.

Private companies are subject to various regulatory and compliance requirements, which can make the capital raising process more complex and expensive.

Despite these challenges, there are several things that companies can do to increase their chances of success in raising capital, which will be shared in the following chapters.

Chapter 2 Strategic Budgeting of Time and Resources

2.1 How Much Time to Budget to Raise Money

Allocating a minimum of 12-18 months towards this endeavour is wise, provided the market conditions are stable. This timeframe lets you identify potential investors, establish strong relationships, and refine your investment proposition. Securing funding often takes longer than initially estimated due to unexpected hurdles and unforeseen events that may delay the process to over a year. Never underestimate the persistence and perseverance required in this journey.

It is rare for an investor to give you all money upfront. They usually will provide an initial investment, with the potential for additional funds as certain milestones are achieved. As you reach important milestones, such as product development or revenue targets, the investor injects more capital into your business.

Breakdown of the typical capital raising timeline

Month 1-2
- *Prepare all the documentation for investors*, including the business plan financial model, pitch deck, executive summary and electronic data room.
- *Prepare and rehearse your pitch.* Your pitch should be clear,

concise, and persuasive. It should highlight your company's unique selling proposition, target market, competitive landscape, financial projections, and exit strategy. Anticipate potential questions that may come up.

- *Identify potential investors.* There are several ways to identify potential investors, such as online databases, industry events, and networking. Social media, like LinkedIn, and AI tools like ChatGPT and Bard have made this process easier. AI tools can churn out lists of investors with reasons why they may be interested.

- *Research investors.* Once you have identified potential investors, take some time to research them. Learn about their investment philosophy, portfolio companies, and recent investments. AI is hugely helpful in explaining why an investor may be interested. You still need to go to each website and check the potential synergies.

- *Develop an investor long list.* Have a long list and a short list. Create a short list of the investors you want to meet with. The shortlist includes investors where the fit seems perfect on paper. Be sure to include all relevant information, such as their name, contact information, investment focus and previous investments. AI can provide you with the CIO/CEO name at each firm. Separately, there are databases you can subscribe to to obtain phone numbers and email addresses.

Month 3-5

- *Reach out to investors.* Start reaching out to investors on your long list. Use the information from your long list to contact investors and introduce your company. You can reach out via email, phone calls, social media, or mutual connections. Craft personalised messages highlighting why you believe they would be interested in your business. I recommend you start with investors not on your shortlist with the view of 'practising'. Their feedback can help you to improve the pitch further before you go to the focus investors on your shortlist.

- *Schedule meetings with the investors* who show genuine interest in your company. Depending on the circumstances, these meetings can be conducted in person or virtually. Send a calendar invitation and follow up with investors regularly to confirm their meeting times. Reconfirm the meeting the day before. Be prepared to answer their questions and discuss your business in more detail.
- *Fine-tune your pitch based on feedback,* making it bulletproof. After each meeting, take note of any feedback or questions from potential investors. Use this feedback to refine and improve your pitch for future presentations.
- *Follow up after each meeting* or interaction with an investor. Send a thank-you note or email summarising key points discussed during the meeting and expressing gratitude for their time and consideration.
- *Continue pitching to additional investors.* Keep reaching out to new potential investors and scheduling meetings as necessary.·

Month 6-12+
- *NDAs signed* by investors followed by preliminary due diligence by the investor before submitting a term sheet.
- *Investment committee approval* before an investor sends a term sheet. The investment team will prepare a proposal to their investment committee to get the go-ahead and start due diligence. This does not mean it is a done deal.
- *Evaluate term sheets and negotiate key terms.* If an investor expresses interest in investing, they may present a term sheet outlining the proposed terms of the investment deal.

Carefully evaluate these offers and negotiate terms that align with your company's goals.·

- *Conduct a due diligence process with the selected investor(s).* Once you have agreed on terms with an investor, they will typically conduct due diligence on your company before finalising the investment agreement. Be prepared to provide the necessary documentation and answer any additional questions they may have. You will be asked hundreds of questions. Investors will end up knowing your business better than you do. You often will get excellent feedback during this process to help further improve your business. Be patient. At times, you may feel the Q&A is never-ending.

- *Finalise legal documentation for investment agreement(s).* Work closely with legal professionals to finalise all documents related to the investment agreement(s) reached with selected investors (s).·

- *Close funding round(s) and secure investments.* Complete the funding round with all legalities sorted out by securing investments from the selected investor(s). This may involve signing investment agreements and transferring funds.· Investors often adopt a strategic approach to allocating their funds, preferring to invest in stages as key milestones are achieved. This approach allows them to carefully assess the progress and potential of the investment before committing additional capital. By investing in increments, investors mitigate risks and ensure that their funds are deployed judiciously. This method also allows both parties to build trust and establish a long-term partnership.

- *Celebrate and communicate the successful fundraising.* Once the funding round is closed, celebrate the achievement with your team and stakeholders. Additionally, communicate the news to your existing investors, employees, customers, and other relevant parties.

- If the investor pulls out, you will be set back by a few months. There are many reasons why an investor may pull out at the last minute, and we will touch on these in a later chapter.

Keep in mind that this timeline is intended as a general reference. The duration of your company's capital raising process may differ depending on the specific circumstances and market conditions. Currently, investors expect businesses to need up to 24 months of runway.

The cycles for raising capital have become longer, sometimes taking a year or more. With the determination and passion of your team, you can overcome any challenges that come your way regarding the timeline. Remember that achieving success is not about rushing through the process but staying committed for the long haul. Stay motivated and dedicated; your company's capital raising efforts will eventually pay off.

2.2 What Causes Delays

Be prepared for many delays

Although AI has made it easier to identify investor names to pitch to, several factors can cause delays in the capital raising process in normal market conditions. Here are some of the most common ones that CEOs often overlook when setting a time frame for a capital raise.

Investors will not drop everything to focus on your proposal. It may take a month before you get an investor's attention. They may be on holiday, or they may be busy closing another transaction. After you have their attention, setting up a first call or meeting may take time, as their diaries can get very full. From first outreach to a meeting or call can take two months.

The company itself can also be a factor in the length of the capital raising process. If the company is not well-prepared, it may take longer to get through the due diligence process and negotiations.

Getting approval from an investment committee may take a week or can take as long as a month. The investment team will need time to prepare their proposal to the investment committee. The investment committee agenda may be full, and they may not be meeting every week.

Due diligence is the process by which investors investigate a company before investing. This process can be time-consuming, as it may involve reviewing financial statements, conducting site visits, and interviewing management. Once investors have completed their due diligence, they will enter negotiations with the company to finalise the terms of the investment. Negotiations can be protracted, as investors want to get a good deal.

In some cases, investments may require regulatory approval. This can add another layer of complexity to the process, as it may involve filing paperwork with government agencies and waiting for responses.

Factors contributing to the lengthening of capital raising cycles

- *Increased Due Diligence:* Investors have become more cautious, especially amid economic uncertainties. They conduct thorough due diligence to mitigate risks, prolonging the time required for decision-making. They do not fear missing out and will take longer to complete their due diligence at leisure.

- *Rising Regulatory Scrutiny:* Stringent regulatory requirements and compliance checks have become more prevalent. Private companies must navigate complex regulatory landscapes, contributing to extended cycles as they ensure alignment with legal frameworks.
- *Market Volatility:* Economic uncertainties and market fluctuations can lead investors to a wait-and-see approach. They may delay investment decisions until they have a clearer understanding of market trends and potential risks.
- *Sophistication of Investment Strategies:* Investors are becoming more sophisticated, employing complex investment strategies. Evaluating and aligning these strategies with a company's goals can extend the time needed to secure investments.
- *Increased Investor Scrutiny:* Investors now scrutinise financial metrics and non-financial aspects such as environmental, social, and governance (ESG) factors. Meeting these diverse criteria demands additional time and effort from companies.
- *Greater Emphasis on Sustainability:* Companies with a strong emphasis on sustainability and ethical practices may attract investors with similar values. However, the due diligence process in these cases can be more exhaustive, lengthening the capital raising cycle.
- *Rise of Pre-Seed and Seed Funding Rounds*: The emergence of pre-seed and seed funding rounds has introduced additional stages in the capital raising process. Companies often go through multiple rounds before securing significant investment, extending the overall cycle.
- *Complex Deal Structures*: Investors may seek more complex deal structures, such as convertible notes or SAFE (Simple Agreement for Future Equity) instruments. Negotiating and

finalising these structures can elongate the capital raising process.

- *Global Economic Factors:* Economic conditions, both domestically and globally, play a significant role. Periods of economic uncertainty or downturns can make investors more cautious, leading to prolonged decision-making processes.
- *Increased Competition:* The growing number of startups seeking investment has intensified competition. Investors have more options, and companies may need to work harder to differentiate themselves, resulting in extended capital raising cycles. Additionally, when liquidity dries up, there are fewer active investors, and many investors reserve capital for their existing investments, which means there is more competition.
- *Companies are often too slow to adjust their valuation down in a bear market or recession:* This can make it harder to attract investors versus the competition that has cut its valuation. They may be overconfident in their business and believe they are worth more than the market will pay. They may be afraid of scaring away investors by lowering their valuation, or they may be reluctant to admit that their business is not worth as much as they thought.
- *Impact of Technology and Information Accessibility:* While technology has streamlined many processes, the increased accessibility of information also means that investors can conduct more in-depth research. This can lead to more prolonged negotiations and a more thorough assessment of a company's prospects.

Private companies must approach extended capital raising cycles with strategic foresight, patient persistence, and unwavering preparation to succeed. The key to success lies in cultivating strong relationships with potential investors, fostering an environment of transparency, and proactively addressing their concerns. With these methods in place, the challenges of a longer capital raising timeline can be met with ease and grace. While raising funds within three months may be the exception, the potential for success is boundless with the right attitude, approach, and commitment. Let's aim high, stay focused, and reap the rewards of a successful funding journey! You will fail again and again; keep going.

Tips for reducing the amount of time it takes to raise money

Investors are busy, so they do not have time to listen to a long-winded pitch. Be sure to have a clear and concise pitch highlighting your business's most critical aspects. The investor will move on to the next proposal if your pitch is too complicated.

Have all documents prepared, including FAQs and the electronic data room. Often, the company delays the due diligence process as they are unprepared and require time to collect and collate the requested information.

Do not waste your time pitching to investors uninterested in your company or industry. Be sure to target the right investors with a track record of investing in similar companies.

During a downturn, many investors engage in window dressing and may not openly acknowledge their lack of liquidity for additional investments. You may be barking up the wrong tree and wasting time.

Investors will anticipate discussing the terms of the investment. Be prepared to compromise certain aspects, but avoid relinquishing too much equity or control over your company. Flexibility regarding your company's valuation will be particularly important in a declining market.

Capital raising is a numbers game. The more investors you pitch to, the more likely you find one willing to invest in your company.

By following these tips, you can reduce the time it takes to raise money from investors. However, it is essential to remember that capital raising will still be time-consuming. Be patient and persistent; eventually, you will find the right investors for your company. Do not rely on one investor. Ensure you have a backup if your investor pulls out at the last minute. Learn as you progress. You will start to understand which investors like what you do and why. You can then start to focus on finding more investors with similar profiles.

Best and worst times for a capital raising campaign

Timing plays a crucial role in attracting investors and maximising their engagement.

Be mindful of holidays that may affect investor activity. For example, during Christmas, Chinese New Year, and Ramadan, many investors in the relevant jurisdictions tend to take time off or have reduced availability. Therefore, launching a capital raising campaign or a roadshow during these periods might not yield the desired results due to reduced investor attention. Many will be out of the office. You may decide to focus on the Middle East in December, as they generally do not celebrate Christmas.

Additionally, the summer months are generally considered a quieter period in terms of business activity for many investors. It is wise to consider this when planning your capital raise, as you may encounter challenges in capturing attention and securing commitments during this time. Investors will continue due diligence over the summer months but usually do not start work on new deals as most of the team, especially the decision-makers, will be out of the office during the summer months.

Timing your fundraising efforts around September and mid-January tends to be best. The post-summer period allows potential investors to refocus their attention on new opportunities after returning from vacations or extended breaks. Similarly, mid-January offers a window as the quiet period over Christmas begins transitioning into increased market activity.

Considering all these factors will help you strategically plan your capital raise for maximum impact and engagement from potential investors.

2.3 What are the Costs to Consider

Estimating the costs associated with raising capital is an essential aspect of financial planning for any business. It's crucial to note that these cost estimates can vary significantly based on several factors. These factors include the complexity of your fundraising efforts, your geographic location, the specific professionals or service providers you engage, and the size of your capital raise. As such, consider these estimates as general ranges rather than fixed numbers. Here are some key expenses you should be aware of when embarking on a capital-raising journey:

- *Accounting Fees:* You will need an accountant to assist you in preparing financial statements and other financial documents for potential investors. The cost of accounting services can vary depending on the size and complexity of your business.
- *Consulting and Advisory Services:* Depending on your specific needs, you may require specialized consulting or

advisory services during the capital raising process. This can include hiring marketing consultants, public relations firms, or strategic advisors, which can add to your overall expenses.

- *Investment Banking Fees:* If you choose to work with an investment banker or a third-party introducer to connect you with potential investors and raise capital, you'll need to pay them a fee. These fees may include retainers and success fees, typically spanning up to six months, and success fees calculated as a percentage of the total amount raised. These percentages often range from 5% to 10% or even more.

- *Valuation Firm:* If you plan to issue equity or convertible securities, you may need to engage an independent valuation firm to determine your company's fair market value. This valuation can significantly impact the terms of your investment and the price at which you sell equity.

- *Marketing and Advertising:* You may need to allocate funds for marketing and advertising to promote your capital raise to potential investors. The costs associated with these efforts can vary based on the scale and scope of your marketing campaign.

- *Printing and Copying:* For investor meetings and presentations, you'll likely need to print and copy investment materials like your pitch deck and financial statements. Costs here depend on the volume of copies required.

- *Database Providers:* If you use third-party database providers offering investor contact data, like Pitchbook, be prepared for potentially substantial costs, often running into tens of thousands of dollars.

- *Professional Advice*: Consider seeking professional advice on presenting to investors effectively, as this can enhance your fundraising efforts.
- *Travel and Event Expenses:* While many investor interactions occur virtually, you may still need to travel to meet with potential investors or host events like investor dinners. Costs can vary depending on the number of investors involved and the location of these meetings. Whenever possible, consider targeting local investors to minimize travel expenses.
- *Compliance and Regulatory Expenses:* Depending on your location and the nature of your capital raise, you may incur expenses related to compliance with securities regulations. This can include fees associated with filing securities documents, conducting background checks on investors, and legal expenses to ensure your offering complies with relevant securities laws.
- *Legal Fees:* To draft and negotiate essential investment documents such as your term sheet and securities purchase agreement, you'll need to hire a lawyer. Legal fees can vary based on the complexity of your raise and the experience of the attorney you engage.

The costs associated with raising capital can accumulate quickly. Therefore, proper planning, budgeting, and negotiation of fees are essential for managing these expenses effectively and ensuring the financial viability of your capital raising campaign. It's crucial to remain flexible and adaptable, as actual costs will depend on your unique circumstances and the professionals and services you engage. Be prepared to adjust your budget as needed, and always have a contingency plan in place in case you cannot raise the desired capital.

Chapter 3 Preparing the Capital Raise

3.1 Preparing to Raise Capital

If you fail to prepare, you prepare to fail. This chapter will cover the steps CEOs must take to prepare to raise capital, such as developing a business plan, creating a pitch deck, and an executive summary. Additionally, the frequently asked questions should be anticipated, and an electronic data room should be set up, ready for when an investor starts the due diligence. Assuming you already have a website, the following needs to be prepared:

- **Pitch deck -** A pitch deck is a presentation that CEOs use to introduce their business to potential investors. The pitch deck should highlight the company's unique value proposition, target market, financial projections, and management team. It should be no more than 12-15 pages.
- **Executive Summary -** An Executive Summary is often overlooked. In this era of short attention span, having a 1-2 page executive summary is crucial.
- **Business plan and financial model -** A business plan is a document that outlines a company's goals, strategies, and financial projections.
- **Visual material -** Short videos, 3-6 minutes long, are a helpful way to introduce a company and its products or services.
- **Frequently Asked Questions -** FAQs are for internal use, anticipating potential investor questions and preparing all

the answers in writing. As new questions come up, you add them to the FAQs.

- **The Electronic Data Room (EDR) -** Investors will conduct due diligence on a company before they invest. This is a process of investigating the company's finances, management team, and business model. CEOs should be prepared to answer any questions that investors may have. There are two due diligence phases: the preliminary and the post-term sheet due diligence. The EDR contains all the information investors want to see when they enter due diligence. You can split it into Level 1 access for preliminary due diligence and Level 2 for full due diligence.
- **Valuation -** CEOs must have a realistic understanding of their company's valuation before capital raising. This will help them to close the deal. Too often, CEOs have inflated views of the valuation.
- **Compliance with regulation -** We will touch on this in a later chapter. It is not limited to regulation. Investors will screen for compliance with ESG, SDGs, Climate Change, Net Zero, Inclusion and Diversity, anti-bribery, disclaimers and more.

3.2 The Pitch Deck

When a CEO raises money for their company, the pitch deck is one of the most important tools. This presentation is a slide deck designed to give potential investors a high-level overview of the company, its product or service, its market, and its team. It usually will be between 12-15 pages.

A well-crafted pitch deck is the foundation for securing a company's funding to grow and succeed. An investment deck is different from a corporate deck. The corporate deck describes the business. The investment pitch deck sells the investment opportunity.

There is no one-size-fits-all, as the specific content of a pitch deck will vary depending on the company, the stage of development and the industry in which it operates.

Tips to help create a pitch deck

Start with a strong introduction. The first few slides of your pitch deck should introduce your company, its product or service, and its target market. Be sure to clearly articulate the problem that your company solves and how your solution is unique and valuable.

Compelling Storytelling: Infuse the pitch deck with a captivating narrative that resonates with investors on an emotional level. Connect with their aspirations and showcase how your company aligns with their vision for the future.

Data-Driven Approach: Supplement all your claims with solid data and evidence. Present key metrics, market research findings, and customer testimonials to substantiate your assertions and establish credibility.

Focus on the market opportunity: Investors want to invest in companies with large and growing addressable markets. Be sure to highlight your target market's size and growth potential in your pitch deck.

Explain your business model: How does your company make money? What are your revenue streams and cost structure? Investors want to understand how your company will generate a return on their investment.

Traction and Milestones: Showcase your company's progress and achievements. Demonstrate traction through early customer acquisition, partnerships, or industry recognition.

Competitive Analysis: Identify your direct and indirect competitors in the market. Highlight your unique selling propositions (USPs) and competitive advantages that set you apart.

Highlight your team: Investors also invest in the company's team. Be sure to highlight the experience and expertise of your team members in your pitch deck.

Be clear about your ask. How much money are you raising, and how do you plan to use it? Investors want to know you have a clear plan for using their money.

Exit Strategy: Provide investors with a clear understanding of your company's potential exit strategy. Outline potential acquisition scenarios, initial public offerings (IPOs), or strategic partnerships that could lead to a successful exit for investors.

Visual Appeal: Ensure the pitch deck is appealing and easy to follow. Use high-quality images, graphics, and charts to communicate your message effectively. Do not overcrowd the slides. If one of the slides is too complicated, the investor will give up and close the deck.

Be concise and to the point: Aim for a pitch deck that is no more than 10-12 slides long. Investors are busy and do not have time to listen to a long presentation.

Use clear and concise language: Avoid jargon and technical terms your audience may not understand. Write as if you are pitching to a twelve-year-old.

What to include on each slide

Slide 1: Title slide
- Ensure the company name and logo are prominent and visually appealing.
- Craft a tagline that succinctly captures the essence of your company's value proposition.
- Include the names and titles of the key presenters to establish credibility.

Slide 2: Executive Summary

Slide 3: Problem
- identify the problem you are addressing, emphasising its significance and impact.
- Quantify the problem's scope using relevant data or statistics to underscore its urgency.
- Provide concrete examples or case studies illustrating the problem's real-world consequences.

Slide 4: Solution
- Introduce your solution in a way that directly addresses the problem highlighted in the previous slide. Explain how your solution effectively tackles the root cause of the problem, not just the symptoms. Emphasise the unique aspects of your solution that differentiate it from alternatives.
- For tech startups or companies with a significant focus on product innovation, outline the current state of the product, any proprietary technology, and future development plans.
- If applicable, a section on the company's intellectual property, like patents, trademarks, or unique business processes, would be valuable, especially for tech or R&D-focused companies.

Slide 5: Market
- Clearly define your target market, specifying the demographics, needs, and pain points. Quantify the market size using credible market research data to demonstrate its potential. Show how the company is positioned to capitalise on future trends.
- Analyse the competitive landscape, identifying key competitors and their strengths and weaknesses. Highlight your company's competitive advantages and how it stands

out in the market.
- If the company operates in a heavily regulated industry, address how it complies with regulations and any upcoming regulatory challenges.

Slide 6: Business model
- Clearly illustrate how your business model creates value for customers and investors.
- Explain how your company generates revenue, outlining the specific sources of income. Describe your cost structure, providing transparency into your expenses and profitability.
- Demonstrate a clear path to profitability, explaining how your business model will deliver returns to investors.

Slide 7: Team and Board
- Showcase the expertise and experience of your executive team members and the Board, highlighting their relevant skills and accomplishments. Highlight the company's commitment to diversity and inclusion, showing a progressive and forward-thinking company culture.
- Emphasise the team's passion and dedication to the company's mission and vision. Convince investors that your team can execute your business plan effectively.

Slide 8: Traction
- Highlight key milestones and achievements that demonstrate your company's progress.
- Showcase customer acquisition or revenue growth metrics to validate your solution's impact.
- Demonstrate real-world application, share testimonials and customer satisfaction with case studies in the Annex.
- Showcase strategic partnerships, collaborations, or endorsements, if any, to demonstrate industry acceptance

and potential for growth through alliances. Emphasise any industry recognition or awards received to enhance your credibility.

Slide 9: Sustainability and Social Impact

- For companies whose product or business model has a sustainability angle or social impact, including this information can be appealing, especially to investors focused on ethical and sustainable investing.

Slide 10: Financials

- Present clear and concise financial projections for the next few years. Include key financial metrics such as revenue, growth rates, and profitability targets.
- Explain how the projected financials align with your company's growth strategy and funding requirements.
- Discuss risk mitigation strategies. Investors appreciate a realistic view of the business's challenges and how the team plans to handle them.

Slide 11: The Ask and Use of Funds

- Clearly state the specific action you are requesting from investors. Make your call to action compelling and easy to understand.
- Consider providing multiple options for engagement, such as investment, partnership, or customer acquisition.
- Outline the ask and the use of funds. Clearly state the funding you seek and how you plan to use the funds. Provide a detailed breakdown of how the investment will be allocated to various aspects of your business.

Slide 12: The Exit Scenarios

- Outline your plan for exiting the business, potentially

through an acquisition, initial public offering (IPO), or strategic partnership.

• Explain how this strategy will provide returns for investors.

Slide 13: Conclusion

• Reiterate the key selling points. Reiterate your company's potential and the value it offers to investors.

Slide 14: Thank you and contact details

Annex: The Annex is used for more complex slides to further detail and support the claims in the deck. You can include case studies. If applicable, a slide dedicated to the technology behind the product or service, especially for tech-focused companies.

Vary the content depending on the stage of development

Your pitch deck should look different when raising capital, depending on your stage of development. Your pitch deck's content, focus, and emphasis will vary based on whether you're in the early stage, growth stage, or later stage of your business. A general guideline for how your pitch deck should differ at each stage:

Early-stage (Seed or Pre-Seed)

• *Emphasis on Vision and Problem-Solution Fit:* At this stage, investors are often more interested in your vision, the problem you're solving, and your initial solution. Your deck should focus on the market opportunity, the problem statement, and how your product or service addresses that problem.

- *Product Prototype or MVP:* Highlight any early-stage product prototypes or minimum viable products (MVPs) to demonstrate your progress.
- *Team:* Emphasize your team's expertise, passion, and commitment. Early-stage investors often bet on the team as much as the idea.
- *Market Validation:* If you have any early traction, user feedback, or customer testimonials, showcase them.
- *Financial Projections:* While projections may be more speculative at this stage, include them to provide a glimpse of your growth potential.
- *Ask:* Clearly state what you're seeking regarding funding and how you plan to use it for further development.

Growth-Stage (Series A and Beyond)
- *Focus on Traction and Metrics:* Investors at this stage will want to see evidence of growth, revenue, and a clear path to scaling. Highlight key performance metrics, such as user acquisition, revenue, customer retention, and market share.
- *Market Expansion:* Explain how you plan to expand into new markets or customer segments.
- *Competitive Advantage:* Showcase your competitive moat, whether it's through technology, network effects, intellectual property, or other barriers to entry.
- *Team and Execution:* Highlight your team's ability to execute your growth plans and manage a scaling organisation.
- *Financials:* Provide more detailed and conservative financial projections and a breakdown of how you intend to use the funding to achieve your growth targets.
- *Investor Terms:* Discuss valuation, investment terms, and proposed exit strategies.

Later-Stage (Series C and Beyond)

- *Scale and Expansion:* Focus on your global expansion plans, potential mergers and acquisitions, and how you intend to dominate your market.
- *Financial Performance:* Provide in-depth financial data, including historical financials, burn rate, cash flow analysis, and profitability metrics.
- *Exit Strategy:* Outline your long-term exit strategy, whether it's an IPO, acquisition, or other means.
- *Market Leadership:* Emphasize your position as an industry leader and the impact of your product or service.
- *Investor Relations:* Discuss how you plan to engage with investors and provide ongoing updates.

3.3 The Executive Summary

The benefits of having an executive summary

A pitch deck is a presentation that you will use to pitch your company to potential investors. The purpose of a pitch deck is to provide investors with a detailed overview of your business, including your product, market, team, financials, and exit strategy.

An executive summary is a document that provides a high-level overview of your business plan and pitch. It should be clear, concise, and persuasive and no more than two pages. An executive summary aims to pique potential investors' interest and encourage them to read your pitch deck.

The executive summary is shared before the pitch deck is shared. It is the first thing many investors will see. It is your chance to make a first impression and convince investors to learn more about your company.

Investors are busy, so they do not have time to read through extended business plans or pitch decks to determine the offering. An executive summary gives them a quick and easy way to learn about your company and decide whether they want to learn more.

An executive summary should summarise the key points of your business plan or pitch deck. This makes it easy for investors to understand your business and to remember why they should invest in your company.

If your executive summary is well-written and persuasive, investors will want to learn more about your company. This will increase the chances of them reading your entire pitch deck and considering your investment opportunity.

The investors can use the summary to communicate with their seniors and the investment committee. It ensures that they correctly relay the message internally. It gives the investor key details to include in an internal note to their investment committee.

How to write an executive summary

An executive summary should be clear, concise, and persuasive. It should also be well-written and free of errors. It includes most items from the pitch deck, condensed to 1-2 pages. Here are some tips for writing an executive summary, which can be adjusted depending on the company's development stage.

At the top, you write 'Executive Summary' and company name. You can have a column on the left, one-third of the width of the page, with all the numbers and the main section on the right, two-thirds of the width of the page, telling the story.

Start with a strong introduction. Introduce your company and its product or service clearly and concisely. Highlight your unique value proposition. What makes your company different from the competition? What problem do you solve for your customers? Address your target market. Who are your ideal customers? How big is your addressable market? Discuss your business model. How does your company make money? Outline the traction. Highlight your team's experience and expertise. Why is your team the right team to build this company? Share a snapshot of your financial projections. What is your projected revenue and profitability? Include the ask and use of funds. Outline your exit strategy. How do you plan to exit the business and return capital to your investors?

3.4 Visual Material

Advantages of short videos

In an era where consumers are bombarded with information, a short video can capture and hold attention better than long-form content. Videos, particularly short ones, tend to have higher engagement rates. They are more likely to be watched in full, shared, liked, and commented on. Videos generate 1,000% more shares than text and images combined. Videos are more stimulating and can hold people's attention longer.

People are more likely to watch a video than read a block of text. Short videos can convey messages more efficiently than text or static images. A well-made video can simplify complex information, making it more accessible to a broader audience.

Videos are easy to share on social media and other online platforms. This can help you reach a wider audience and raise more money. These videos can be used across various platforms

— from a company's website to social media channels like YouTube, Instagram, and LinkedIn.

Videos can evoke emotions through storytelling, visuals, and music, creating a stronger connection with the audience. Stories are a powerful way to connect with people on an emotional level. Videos allow you to tell your organisation's story compellingly and memorably.

When people can see and hear from the people running your organisation, they are more likely to trust you. Videos can help you put a human face on your organisation and show credibility and trustworthiness.

For companies, especially those with physical products or visually demonstrable services, videos can effectively showcase features and benefits.

Through consistent style, tone, and messaging, short videos help reinforce brand identity and increase brand recognition.

Tips for creating effective capital raising videos

Given the short duration, the video should have a clear and focused message. Avoid covering too much; highlight the most critical aspects of the company, product, or service. Use storytelling to make the video compelling. A narrative that resonates with the target audience can significantly enhance the impact. Aim for videos that are no longer than six minutes long. A short video can capture and hold attention better than long-form content. Videos, particularly short ones, tend to have higher engagement rates. They are more likely to be watched in full, shared, liked, and commented on.

The quality of your visuals will reflect on your organisation. Make sure to use high-quality footage, graphics, and sound. Invest in good production quality, including clear visuals, professional editing, and sound quality. Poor production can detract from the message and harm the brand image.

How to allocate the time in your video

- Introduction (30 seconds): Briefly introduce your company, its product or service, and its unique value proposition.
- Problem (1 minute): Clearly articulate the problem your company solves. Why is this problem important? How big is the problem?
- Solution (1 minute): Introduce your company's product or service. How does your solution solve the problem identified in the previous slide? What makes your solution unique and valuable?
- Market (30 seconds): Define your target market and highlight its size and growth potential.
- Business model (30 seconds): Explain how your company makes money. What are your revenue streams and cost structure? How will you generate a return on investment for investors?
- Team (30 seconds): Highlight the experience and expertise of your team members. Why are you the right team to execute your company's vision?
- Traction (30 seconds): Highlight your company's progress. This could include customer acquisition, revenue growth, or product development milestones.
- Financials (30 seconds): Present your financial projections for the next few years. How much money are you raising, and how do you plan to use it?
- Call to action (30 seconds): Clearly state what you want investors to do. Are you asking them to invest in your company? Are you asking them to sign up for your beta

program? Are you asking them to connect you with potential customers?
- Thank you (15 seconds): Thank investors for their time and consideration.

3.5 Business Plan and Financial Model

A business plan is a comprehensive overview of your company's goals, strategies, and financial projections. Investors will scrutinise the business plan to assess the company's potential for success and make informed investment decisions.

What should be included in a business plan

- *Executive Summary:* This concise overview is the first impression, highlighting your company's key strengths, objectives, and financial projections. Capture investors' attention with a clear and compelling summary of your business proposition.
- *Company Description:* Provide a detailed description of your company, including its history, mission, vision, and core values. Explain what differentiates your company from competitors and how you plan to establish a unique position in the market.
- *Market Analysis:* Conduct thorough market research to understand the industry landscape, target audience, and competitive environment. Identify your target market segments, analyse market trends and behaviour, and assess key competitors' strengths and weaknesses.
- *Products or Services:* Describe your products or services in detail, emphasising their unique features, benefits, and value proposition. Explain how your offerings address

customer needs and solve market problems.

- *Marketing and Sales Strategy:* Outline your marketing and sales strategies to effectively reach your target market and generate revenue. Describe your pricing strategy, promotional channels, and sales process.
- *Operations Plan:* Explain how you will deliver your products or services to customers. Detail your operational processes, supply chain management, and logistics plans. Describe your production capabilities, quality control measures, and inventory management strategies.
- *Management Team:* Highlight the expertise and experience of your management team. Provide detailed information about each key member's qualifications, background, and track record.
- *Financial Projections:* Present realistic financial projections, including revenue forecasts, expense breakdowns, and cash flow statements. Demonstrate your understanding of financial metrics and ability to effectively manage the company's finances.
- *Funding Requirements:* Clearly state the funding you seek and how you plan to use the funds. Explain your funding timeline and intended use of the capital.
- *Exit Strategy:* Outline your plans for future growth and potential exit opportunities for investors. Discuss the possibility of an IPO, acquisition, or other forms of value realisation.
- *Risk Assessment:* Identify and evaluate potential risks associated with your business operations, including market risks, competitive threats, and financial challenges. Demonstrate your understanding of risk mitigation strategies. Include different business scenarios (like best-case, worst-case, and most likely case) to showcase preparedness for various market conditions.

- *Intellectual Property:* If applicable, describe your intellectual property assets, including patents, trademarks, or copyrights. Explain how you protect your intellectual property rights and how they contribute to your company's competitive advantage.
- *Appendix:* Include supporting documents that provide additional context or strengthen your business plan, such as letters of intent, market research reports, or customer testimonials.

A well-crafted business plan is a persuasive tool to attract investors and secure funding. Tailor your plan to the specific interests of your target investors, highlighting the aspects that resonate with their investment criteria and risk tolerance.

What goes into a financial model

Financial models are an essential tool for projecting future cash flows and profitability. They help companies understand their financial position and make informed decisions about their future. Financial models can forecast revenue and expenses and project cash flow from operations. It can analyse the impact of different capital investments and evaluate a new project's potential return on investment (ROI). It also assesses a business's financial risks.

There are many different financial models, but they all share the same basic elements: inputs, formulas and outputs. Inputs are the assumptions and data used to build the model. Formulas are the mathematical equations that are used to calculate the outputs. The outputs are the model's results, such as projected cash flows, profitability, and ROI.

Financial models can be complex and challenging to build but invaluable for companies making critical financial decisions. Financial models help companies make better decisions about their future by clearly understanding their financial position and the potential impact of different options. Financial models help companies improve transparency by providing a clear and concise way to communicate their financial plans to investors, lenders, and other stakeholders. Financial models can help companies reduce risk by identifying potential financial problems early on and helping them develop contingency plans.

Financial models are not without their limitations. They are based on assumptions, and the accuracy of the results depends on the quality of the inputs and the assumptions. Despite the limitations, financial models are essential for any company making important financial decisions.

The most common financial models used by businesses

- *Three-statement model:* This model includes the balance sheet, income statement, and cash flow statement. It can be used to forecast a company's financial performance over time.
- *Discounted cash flow (DCF) model:* This model calculates the present value of a future stream of cash flows. It can be used to value a company or an investment.
- *Budgeting model:* This model plans a company's financial performance over a specific period.
- *Sensitivity analysis:* This technique assesses how sensitive a financial model is to changes in its inputs and assumptions.

Investor expectations of the financial model

- *Comprehensive:* The model should include all relevant financial statements, including the income statement, balance sheet, and cash flow statement. It should also include projections for future performance based on assumptions about revenue growth, expenses, and cash flow.

- *Transparent:* The model should be transparent and easy to understand. Investors should be able to see the assumptions made and understand how the model works. This will help them to assess the risks and rewards of investing in the company.

- *Historical data or benchmarking:* Financial models should be grounded in historical data and industry benchmarks to provide a realistic context for projections. Models that lack historical data or fail to compare performance to industry peers raise concerns about the model's reliability.

- *Realistic Assumptions:* The assumptions used in the model should be realistic and achievable. Investors will be looking for a model that shows a clear path to profitability, and they will be sceptical of models that make unrealistic assumptions about growth or margins.

- *Revenue model:* A clear understanding of the company's revenue model and how it will generate revenue. Investors will be cautious of models that project unrealistic revenue growth without considering market saturation, competition, or potential economic downturns.

- *Realistic estimate of expenses:* A detailed breakdown of the company's expenses and how they will be managed. Models that consistently underestimate expenses or fail to account for potential costs can lead to overstated profitability. Investors will want a comprehensive breakdown of expenses and a realistic assessment of cost management strategies.

- *Realistic cash flow forecasts:* A realistic assessment of the company's cash flow needs and how they will be financed. Cash flow is a critical factor in assessing a company's financial health. Models that project unrealistic cash flow patterns, such as consistently negative cash flow from operations, can raise concerns about the company's ability to meet its financial obligations.
- *Sensitivity analysis:* Sensitivity analysis is a technique used to assess how changes in key assumptions affect the financial model's outcomes. Investors will want to see evidence of sensitivity analysis to understand the model's robustness and the potential impact of different market scenarios.
- *Consistent with the company's narrative:* The financial model should be consistent with the company's business plan and narrative. Investors will want to see that the model tells the same story about the company's future as the business plan.
- *Well-documented:* The model should be well-documented, with clear explanations of the assumptions and calculations that have been made. This will help investors to understand the model and to ask informed questions. Do not dump ten different models on the investors' desks for them to figure out. Make it easy for them to analyse your numbers and include everything in one spreadsheet.
- *Free of errors:* It is embarrassing when investors pick up on errors in formulas and numbers. Do your best to ensure the numbers are the same in all your documentation. Inconsistencies confuse investors.

Make sure the numbers are the same in all your documentation. In addition to these general requirements, investors will also be looking for specific things in a company's financial model, depending on the stage of the company and the type of investment. For example, early-stage companies must show strong revenue growth projections, while later-stage companies must show a path to profitability.

3.6 Documenting Anticipated FAQs

Anticipated Frequently Asked Questions (FAQs) are a great way to prepare to provide potential investors with information about your company and its capital raising process.

The benefits of documenting FAQs

It helps to answer investors' questions upfront. Investors will have many questions about your company and its capital raising process. By documenting FAQs, you can answer these questions upfront and save time during capital raising. It also ensures you provide accurate and complete information to investors.

It ensures a quick turnaround. Delays in answering questions can be detrimental. Quickly responding to questions will make a good impression on investors.

It helps the management team think through aspects of the business. FAQs may spark a discussion internally and help clarify a company's strategy.

Sharing the FAQs with everyone involved in the capital raise ensures everyone gives the same answer. Investors do not like inconsistencies and pick up on them. Train everyone in your company to give the same answers. Often, an investor will ask the same question to different people in the company. Having all the answers prepared empowers the team to engage with investors confidently.

It shows that you are prepared. Being well-prepared with documented answers to anticipated questions showcases professionalism. It conveys that your team is thorough, well-organized and understands the business. This can increase your chances of success when raising money.

It builds trust with investors. You can build trust with them by being transparent and providing investors with clear and concise answers to their questions. It shows you are ready to address any concerns they may have. This can make them more likely to invest in your company.

How to document FAQs

When documenting FAQs, answer the most common questions investors ask. You can gather these questions by talking to other entrepreneurs who have raised money, reading articles about capital raising, and asking your team members what questions they think investors will ask. Once you have a list of questions, start drafting answers. Be sure to answer the questions clearly, concisely, and informally. Avoid using jargon or technical terms that investors may not understand. Once you have drafted the answers to the questions, please review them carefully and make any necessary edits. You may also ask a trusted friend or colleague to review the answers and provide feedback.

Some examples of FAQs you may want to include in your documentation: What is your company's mission and vision? What problem does your company solve? Who is your target market? What is your competitive advantage? How do you make money? What are your financial projections? What is your exit strategy? How much money are you raising? How will you use the money you raise? What is your investment timeline? What kind of investors are you looking for? Who are your current investors? What is your planned exit?

Preparing and maintaining an FAQ document is a proactive and strategic step. It helps you address investors' questions efficiently and reinforces your professionalism and commitment to transparency, ultimately contributing to the success of your fundraising efforts. As you engage with investors and gather feedback, you can use their questions and concerns to refine and expand your FAQ document over time. This iterative process can lead to a more comprehensive and effective resource.

3.7 The Electronic Dataroom

Electronic Data Rooms (EDRs) play a vital role in facilitating a smooth and secure exchange of information with potential investors during the capital raising process. These virtual repositories are centralised hubs for storing, organising, and sharing critical documents, promoting transparency and efficiency throughout the due diligence process.

Companies will ask the investor to sign a Non-Disclosure Agreement (NDA) before sharing the password-protected data room. Keep your NDA short, as it may get stuck in the legal department. Investors may sometimes ask you to use their already approved NDA. If it is acceptable to you, signing their NDA will speed up the process. It is not a good idea to waive the NDA. Most investors will appreciate you are taking care that proprietary information does not fall into the wrong hands. Companies have asked for an NDA to be signed before sending the pitch deck. This is a non-starter and does not show appreciation for the competition in the marketplace.

EDRs allow investors to access pertinent information quickly and easily, streamlining the due diligence process and accelerating decision-making. This eliminates the need for sifting through voluminous physical or scattered digital documents.

EDRs provide a secure environment for sensitive financial data and confidential business information, with encryption, access controls, and audit trails. This helps to safeguard sensitive information from unauthorised access. EDRs enable seamless collaboration among stakeholders, including investors, legal teams, and financial advisors. This creates a collaborative environment where information can be shared, reviewed, and discussed in real-time.

EDR administrators can set customisable access levels for different users, ensuring that only authorised individuals can access specific documents. This helps to maintain confidentiality and control the flow of information. EDRs track document versions, changes, and user activities, providing insights into the evolution of documents over time and ensuring that everyone is working with the latest information.

EDRs provide a structured and organised framework for documents, making it easy for investors to navigate through folders and quickly find the information they need. EDRs eliminate the need for physical data rooms, reducing travel expenses and on-site time. This makes the capital raising process more cost-effective and time-efficient for both parties.

The EDRs are an essential tool for businesses that are raising capital. By leveraging an EDR, companies can streamline the due diligence process, build trust with investors, and expedite capital raising while maintaining the highest standards.

Plan for regularly updating the EDR with the latest financials, press releases, or product/service updates to keep potential investors informed.

What goes into an Electronic Data Room

- *Capital Raising Documentation:* Executive Summary and Pitch Deck.
- *Market and competitive analysis:* Market studies, competitor analyses, and marketing strategies.
- *Strategic plans and business model*: Long-term business plans, growth strategies, and the overall business model.
- *Financial documents*: Audited financial statements, income statements, balance sheets, cash flow statements, and financial projections.
- *Cap table:* This document shows the company's ownership structure, including all shareholders' names and percentages.
- *Legal Documents*: contracts, agreements, intellectual property documentation, licenses, and legal obligations or disputes.
- *Intellectual property portfolio:* Patents, trademarks, copyrights, and other intellectual property assets.
- *Operational information:* Details about the company's operations, supply chain, and manufacturing processes.
- *Risk assessments*: Critical documents that identify and evaluate the risks a company faces for all company areas, including financial, legal, operational, compliance, and IT. Risk assessments help companies understand and mitigate risks, improving performance and profitability.
- *Corporate governance documents*: Board meeting minutes, shareholder agreements, and charts on the organisational structure.
- *Compliance records:* Documents demonstrating compliance with industry regulations and legal requirements.
- *Employee and human resources information:* Employee contracts, organisational structure, and HR policies.

- *Management team bios:* This should provide information about the experience and qualifications of the company's management team.
- *IT infrastructure and cybersecurity:* Information on the company's IT systems, cybersecurity measures, and data protection protocols.

Intellectual Property (IP)

The Electronic Dataroom should include information about the company's Intellectual Property (IP). Investors are looking for a company with a strong IP portfolio, especially strong patents, when considering an investment.

Investors look for strong and enforceable patents. This means the patents should be broad enough to cover the company's technology but not so broad that they are invalid. Investors will also want to see that the patents are well-written and that there is no prior art that could invalidate them. Investors like to see the company has a broad IP portfolio covering all its key technologies. This will give the company a wider range of protection from competitors and make it more difficult for them to copy its products or services.

Investors will want to ensure that the company has the freedom to operate its business without infringing on the intellectual property rights of others. This means that the company should have a clear understanding of the IP landscape and that it has taken steps to avoid infringing on the patents of others. Investors like to see that the company has a track record of enforcing its intellectual property rights. This means the company has been willing to take legal action against companies infringing on its patents. A strong track record of IP enforcement will show investors that the company is serious about protecting its intellectual property.

They want to see the company strategically use its IP to advance its business goals. This means the company uses its IP to develop new products and services, enter new markets, and license its technology to other companies.

Investors expect to see a strong IP management team. This team should be responsible for developing and implementing the company's IP strategy and have the expertise to identify, protect, and enforce the company's IP assets. A strong IP portfolio can be a valuable asset, giving investors confidence that the company is well-positioned for long-term success. By developing and protecting its IP assets, a company can increase its chances of attracting investment and achieving its business goals.

The earlier a company builds its IP portfolio, the stronger it will be. This will give the company a head start on its competitors and make it more attractive to investors. Many resources are available to help companies develop and protect their IP assets. Companies should consider seeking professional help from patent attorneys and other IP specialists. IP Law constantly evolves, so companies must stay updated on the latest developments. This will help them avoid infringement and maximise their IP assets.

Employment contracts

Investors may request that key employees sign non-compete clauses to prevent them from taking valuable knowledge and expertise to competitors after leaving the company. This protects the company's competitive advantage and prevents the loss of confidential information.

They may ask all employees to sign confidentiality agreements to protect sensitive company information, such as trade secrets, customer lists, and business plans. This helps to prevent the disclosure of confidential information that could harm the company's competitive position.

Changes may be needed to termination provisions to ensure the company can terminate employees for cause, even if the cause is not explicitly listed in the contract. This gives the company more control over its workforce and allows it to act if an employee's performance or behaviour is detrimental to its success.

Investors may request that employees assign all intellectual property rights they create while working for the company to the company. This ensures that the company owns all innovations and inventions developed by its employees and can protect and commercialise them as needed.

Investors like to see severance packages capped at a reasonable level or tied to the company's financial performance. This helps to control the company's expenses and ensures that severance payments are aligned with the company's financial health.

Investors will want to ensure that key terms in the contract, such as "cause" for termination and "confidential information," are clearly defined to avoid disputes.

Any restrictions on employees, such as non-compete clauses, should be reasonable and not overly broad. Overly restrictive clauses could make it difficult for employees to find new employment after leaving the company, which could lead to legal challenges.

Investors will want to ensure that the employment contracts are fair to employees and do not take advantage of them. This includes providing employees with adequate notice of termination and severance pay and ensuring they can negotiate the terms of their contracts.

Investors review employment contracts carefully to protect their investment and ensure the company's long-term success.

Companies can attract and retain top talent by negotiating fair and reasonable contracts while protecting their sensitive information and intellectual property assets.

EDR selection process: a checklist

By using an EDR, businesses can instil confidence in potential investors: EDRs demonstrate a commitment to transparency and efficiency, which can help to build trust with investors and increase the chances of success. It should significantly expedite the capital raising process: EDRs streamline the due diligence process, allowing investors to access the information they need quickly and easily. It maintains the highest standards of security and confidentiality: EDRs provide a secure environment for sensitive information, helping to protect businesses from potential risks.

Start your EDR selection process by thoroughly researching available options. Create a comprehensive list of candidates. Reviews can provide valuable insights into each platform's user experiences, strengths, and weaknesses. Assess the EDR provider's financial stability and long-term viability. You want to ensure that the platform will be available and supported for the duration of your capital raising efforts. Some providers charge based on usage or data volume, while others may have a subscription-based pricing structure. Consider your requirements, such as document management, security, user access control, and reporting capabilities. Verify that the EDR provider employs robust encryption, access controls, and compliance with industry standards to protect your data from breaches. Test the platform's user interface to ensure it is intuitive and easy to navigate. This will minimise the learning curve for everyone involved. Some EDRs offer customisation options, allowing you to brand the data room with your company's logo and colours. Ensure it can accommodate your company's growth and increasing data storage needs over time. You'll want assurance that your data is safe in case of unforeseen incidents.

Chapter 4 Setting the Valuation

4.1 Setting the Valuation

As the CEO of a private company, one of your most important responsibilities is to set a valuation for your business. This valuation will be used to attract investors, sell shares to employees, and make other important financial decisions.

Raising money from friends, family, and high net worth individuals (HNWI) can sometimes be easier regarding valuation. HNWIs are often more flexible and may be willing to invest based on their personal relationships or belief in the CEO's vision. However, when dealing with institutional investors, the dynamics can change significantly. Institutional investors have fiduciary responsibilities towards their shareholders or clients. This means they must carefully assess any investment opportunity's potential risks and returns. As such, they might negotiate for lower valuations or demand additional protective clauses to safeguard their interests.

When CEOs transition from fundraising among HNWIs to engaging with institutional investors, they must be prepared for more rigorous scrutiny and potentially more challenging negotiations on valuation. CEOS need to understand this shift in dynamics and adapt their strategies accordingly. It may involve a down round. By arming yourself with a valuation analysis, you will have touch points to use in negotiations.

There is no one-size-fits-all answer to how to set a valuation for a private company. The best approach will vary depending on the specific circumstances of your business, such as its industry, stage of growth, and financial performance. However, there are several factors that you should consider when setting a valuation.

4.2 Pre and Post-Money Valuation

Valuation is the process of determining how much a company is worth. The relationship between pre-money and post-money valuation can be expressed by the formula: Post-money valuation = Pre-money valuation + New capital raised.

Pre-money valuation is the value of a company before it raises any new capital. It is calculated by considering the company's assets, liabilities, revenue, and potential for growth. Pre-money valuation determines the percentage of ownership investors will receive for their investment.

Post-money valuation is the value of a company after it raises new capital. It is calculated by adding the pre-money valuation to the amount of new capital raised. Post-money valuation determines the dilution of existing shareholders' ownership.

Dilution is the reduction in ownership percentage that existing shareholders experience when a company raises new capital. Dilution occurs because the new investors receive a share of ownership in the company.

For example, if a company has a pre-money valuation of $10 million and raises $2 million in new capital, its post-money valuation will be $12 million. This means existing shareholders will own 83.3% of the company after the investment, down from 100% before the investment.

4.3 Impact of Convertible Instruments on Valuation

Convertible instruments, such as convertible notes and SAFE (Simple Agreement for Future Equity) agreements, are popular financing options for startups due to their flexibility and relative simplicity. However, they can significantly impact a company's pre-money and post-money valuation, especially when these instruments convert into equity.

Convertible notes are short-term debt instruments that convert into equity, usually at the next financing round. They often include a discount rate and an interest rate. Initially, convertible notes are treated as debt, not affecting the pre-money valuation directly. These notes convert into equity at the time of conversion (usually at the next equity financing round). The number of shares issued depends on the conversion terms, which often include a valuation cap and/or a discount to the price per share paid by new investors. This conversion dilutes existing shareholders and increases the post-money valuation.

A SAFE agreement can be converted into equity at a future date under specific conditions. Unlike convertible notes, SAFEs are not debt and do not accrue interest. Since SAFEs are not debt and do not immediately convert into equity, they do not affect the pre-money valuation at the time of their issuance. SAFEs typically convert into equity during the next financing round based on the agreed-upon terms (which may include valuation caps and discounts). This conversion dilutes the ownership percentage of existing shareholders and thus impacts the post-money valuation.

Both convertible notes and SAFEs dilute existing shareholders' equity when they convert. The conversion terms (like discount rates, valuation caps, and interest rates) can add complexity to valuation calculations. The actual impact on valuation becomes clear only at the time of conversion. Future investors will consider the impact of these convertible instruments on their ownership stake and might negotiate terms accordingly.

4.4 Valuation Methodology

There are many valuation methodologies. Here are the three main ones.

Comparable company analysis

One of the most common ways to value a private company is to compare it to similar public companies. This is known as comparable company analysis (CCA). To conduct a CCA, you must identify a set of public companies like your business in terms of industry, size, growth rate, and profitability. Analyse the valuation multiples of these companies, such as the Price-to-Earnings (P/E) ratio and Enterprise Value-to-EBITDA (EV/EBITDA). You can use their valuation multiples to estimate your company's value by applying them to your company's financial metrics. You may then need to apply a discount or a premium.

Precedent transaction analysis

Another way to value a private company is to look at recent acquisitions of similar private companies. This is known as precedent transaction analysis. To conduct a precedent transaction analysis, you must identify a set of recent acquisitions of private companies that are like your business in terms of industry, size, and growth rate. Once you have identified a set of precedent transactions, you can use the purchase prices to estimate your company's value by applying the multiples paid. You may then need to apply a discount, as this method often includes a control premium, which might not apply to a private company valuation.

Discounted cash flow analysis

If your company is early-stage or has a unique business model, you may need to use discounted cash flow (DCF) analysis to value your business. DCF analysis involves estimating your company's future cash flows and then discounting them back to the present day. DCF analysis aims to calculate the net present value (NPV) of your company's future cash flows. The NPV is then used as an estimate of your company's valuation. This analysis is highly sensitive to assumptions about future performance and the discount rate, making it more subjective. Investors may dispute the appropriate discount rate and the projected cash flows, which can be hard to estimate for startups or highly innovative companies.

What is the best method

The best method for valuing your private company will depend on your company's specific circumstances. If there are several similar public companies, then CCA may be the best method. If there have been recent acquisitions of comparable private companies, then precedent transaction analysis may be the best method. If your company is in the early stage or has a unique business model with no comparable, then DCF analysis may be the best method.

It is important to note that there is no one-size-fits-all approach to valuing a private company. The best approach will vary depending on the specific circumstances of your company.

Determining the appropriate discount to comparable companies is more art than science. Limited financial history, uncertain future cash flows, and the evolving nature of the market can complicate the valuation process. There are several other factors that you should consider when setting a valuation for your private company, such as the quality of your management team, the company's intellectual property, the competitive landscape and the overall economic climate.

Get multiple valuations

If you are unsure how to value your company, consider hiring a professional valuation expert. As your company grows and changes, your valuation must be updated periodically. Do not rely on a single valuation method to determine your company's value; get numerous valuations from different sources. A blend of valuation methods can provide a more balanced view. This will give you a better idea of the range of possible values for your company. Understand the bias of an investment bank. An investment bank often overvalues your business as they are pitching for your IPO business. Be aware that this is not an unbiased opinion. So do not make the mistake of thinking your investment bank's valuation is right and the investor is wrong.

Internal biases toward the valuation

Many deals fall apart because of disagreement on the valuation. Company founders and management teams often have an emotional attachment to their business, leading to overly optimistic projections and valuations. Overestimation of growth prospects, underestimation of risks, and unrealistic financial projections. There is a tendency to rely heavily on an initial piece of information (the "anchor") when making decisions. This could be a previous funding round or a competitor's. It is harder for the CEO to focus on current changed market conditions and the unique aspects of the business rather than relying on past valuations.

Negotiating the valuation with investors

Do not overvalue your company. Investors are sophisticated and can spot an overvalued company from a mile away. They will not even engage and have a meeting. Be realistic when setting your valuation, and be prepared to compromise. The final decision on the discount rate applied to the multiples of comparable companies or purchase prices is usually a negotiation point. Investors typically want to pay a lower valuation than you are asking for because of the biases highlighted. Investors' moods or attitudes towards the market or specific industry sectors can influence valuations. In a bullish market, valuations may be inflated; in a bearish market, they may be undervalued. Investors, especially influential ones, can have biases or agendas that impact valuation. Investors might push for lower valuations to get a larger stake. Understanding their perspective and being prepared with solid data to support your valuation will help you negotiate the best possible price.

4.5 Use of Valuation

Once you have a realistic valuation for your company, you can use it to achieve your business goals. Your valuation can be used to attract investors, sell shares to employees, and make other important financial decisions such as mergers, acquisitions, and exit strategies.

If you want to raise capital, your valuation will determine how much money you can raise and at what price. A higher valuation will allow you to raise more money at a higher price.

Top talent is expensive but essential for your company's success. A higher valuation will allow you to offer top talent competitive salaries and equity packages.

If you plan to exit, your valuation will determine how much money you can make. A higher valuation will allow you to sell your company for a higher price.

4.6 How to Sell a Down Round to Existing Investors

Selling a down round, where a company raises capital at a lower valuation, can be challenging but not impossible. While it may seem daunting to approach existing investors with this news, there are strategies you can employ to navigate this situation effectively. Here's some advice on how to sell a down round in capital raising to your existing investors. Be open and transparent about the reasons behind the lower valuation and the steps you are taking to address them.

Clearly explain how this will ultimately benefit the company's long-term prospects. Emphasise that external factors such as market conditions or industry trends influence the decision for a down round. By illustrating that these circumstances are beyond your control, you position yourself as proactive in adapting to challenges.

Despite the lower valuation, showcase compelling growth opportunities for your business moving forward. Outline strategies for capturing new markets, expanding product lines, or increasing customer acquisition – all of which can inspire investor confidence. Reiterate why your investors initially believed in your company by reminding them of its unique value proposition and competitive advantages. Reinforce how these strengths will enable you to bounce back from setbacks and deliver significant returns over time. To mitigate concerns regarding dilution resulting from additional funding rounds at lower valuations, consider providing investment incentives such as discounted options or other equity grants for existing shareholders.

Personalised discussions allow you to address individual concerns and build rapport with each investor separately. Take the time to understand their perspective and tailor your message accordingly. If possible, secure backing from influential lead investors who have already committed themselves fully despite the down-round scenario; their endorsement can reassure other stakeholders about the viability of future growth.

A clear roadmap illustrates how the injected capital will be utilised to achieve specific milestones and drive the company towards profitability. This demonstrates your commitment to maximising shareholder value despite the temporary setback.

Chapter 5 Embracing ESG and SDGs

5.1 ESG in Capital Raising

Environmental, social, and governance (ESG) factors are becoming increasingly important for investors. In multiple studies, most investors believe ESG factors are essential to their investment decisions. This is good news for CEOs looking to raise money, as ESG-focused companies tend to attract more investment. One study found that ESG-focused companies outperformed the broader market by 5% over ten years.

There are several reasons why investors are drawn to ESG-focused companies. First, ESG-focused companies are often more innovative and resilient. They are also more likely to attract and retain top talent. Second, ESG-focused companies are usually better managed and more transparent. Third, ESG-focused companies are less likely to be involved in scandals or controversies.

Environmental: This includes reducing waste, conserving energy, and using renewable resources. Investors are interested in understanding the environmental impact of a company's operations. This includes resource usage, waste management, pollution control, and conservation efforts. Companies prioritising sustainability and having effective environmental management systems are more likely to attract investment.

Social: This includes treating employees fairly, respecting human rights, and giving back to the community.

Investors also consider the social impact of a company's activities. They want evidence of responsible labour practices, community engagement, and positive societal contributions. Companies that prioritise employee well-being, support local communities and address social issues tend to be viewed favourably by investors.

Governance includes having a solid board of directors, transparent financial reporting, and ethical business practices. Effective governance is crucial for sustainable business growth. Investors seek companies with transparent decision-making processes, strong board structures, ethical business practices, and robust risk management systems. They want assurance that the company is being managed responsibly and with integrity.

How to raise money with an ESG focus

Many investors specialise in investing in ESG-focused companies. CEOs should target these investors when raising money. CEOs should highlight their company's ESG focus when pitching to investors. This will show investors that the company is committed to ESG and that it is a good investment. Investors want to see that companies are transparent about their ESG performance. CEOs should be prepared to answer questions about their company's ESG performance and provide documentation supporting their claims. CEOs can participate in ESG initiatives by participating in industry groups, attending conferences, and supporting charities and nonprofits working on ESG issues. This will help to raise the company's profile in the ESG community and make it more attractive to ESG-focused investors.

By focusing on ESG, CEOs can raise money from more investors and attract more customers. ESG is also good for the bottom line, as ESG-focused companies tend to be more profitable and resilient.

CEOs can demonstrate their commitment to ESG by developing and implementing an ESG policy. This written policy should outline the company's ESG goals and objectives. It should also describe the company's steps to achieve these goals.

CEOs should also consider reporting on their ESG performance. This can be done through an annual sustainability report or a separate ESG report. Reporting on ESG performance can help attract investors and customers interested in supporting ESG-focused companies.

5.2 Diversity and Inclusion

There are several things that private companies can do to create an inclusive capital raising environment.

The first step is to commit clearly to diversity and inclusion at the organisational level. This commitment should be communicated to all employees and advisors and reflected in all aspects of the capital raising process.

Hiring candidates from different backgrounds is a priority when recruiting new employees and advisors. This may involve outreach to minority communities and organisations that serve underrepresented groups.

Provide all employees and advisors with training on diversity and inclusion. This training should cover unconscious bias, inclusive communication, and cultural competency.

Ensure your office is a welcoming and supportive environment for all staff and advisors. This includes creating a space where everyone feels comfortable sharing their ideas and opinions and feels valued and respected.

Be aware of the language in your capital raising materials and communications. Avoid using language that is exclusive or discriminatory. Use inclusive language in your capital raising materials. This includes using gender-neutral language, avoiding stereotypes, and respectful language about people from different backgrounds.

Make your capital raising events and campaigns accessible to everyone. This includes accommodation for disabled people, childcare and transportation assistance, and translation services.

Be respectful of cultural differences. When capital is raised from investors from different cultures, respect their cultural norms and values. This may involve adapting your capital raising approach to fit their culture.

Celebrate diversity. Celebrate the diversity of your capital raising team and your investor base. This can be done through social media, your website, and your capital raising materials.

By creating an inclusive capital raising environment, private companies can attract and retain diverse employees and advisors, build stronger relationships with investors, and enhance their reputation.

Studies have shown that companies with diverse teams will likely raise more capital than those with less diverse teams. In today's competitive job market, top talent seeks to work for companies committed to diversity and inclusion. Studies have ALSO shown that companies with diverse teams perform better than companies with less diverse teams.

Overall, diversity and inclusion are good for business. Private companies can position themselves for success by creating an inclusive capital raising environment.

5.3 SDGs, Climate Change, and Net-Zero

Other crucial sustainability issues, such as the UN Sustainable Development Goals (SDGs), climate change, and achieving net-zero emissions, have also gained significant attention. Investors recognise that addressing these challenges is morally responsible and helps drive long-term business success.

The SDGs provide a comprehensive framework for sustainable development across various sectors like poverty alleviation, gender equality, clean energy access, and more. By aligning with these goals, companies can showcase their commitment to creating positive social and environmental impacts while securing investor trust.

Climate change mitigation efforts have become paramount in recent years due to their potential impact on businesses' resilience and value creation. Investors seek companies that actively manage climate-related risks by setting ambitious goals for reducing greenhouse gas emissions or transitioning towards carbon neutrality. Achieving net-zero emissions has become a key target for organisations across industries as part of their broader climate strategies.

Investors increasingly consider various interconnected factors beyond ESG when making investment decisions. Embracing the UN SDGs while addressing climate change concerns through net-zero commitments alongside diversity and inclusion efforts can enhance companies' attractiveness to forward-thinking investors looking for sustainable growth opportunities.

5.4. Social Impact Investing

Social impact investing (SII) is a growing investment trend, especially among the next generation, focusing on generating positive social and environmental impact alongside financial returns. Impact investors increasingly seek opportunities to invest in businesses and organisations making a positive difference in the world.

Triple Bottom Line (TBL) is a concept that goes beyond the traditional focus solely on financial performance. It incorporates three key dimensions: people, planet, and profit. This framework measures a company's success and sustainability based on social, environmental, and economic factors. The TBL encourages a holistic evaluation of a company's impact on society, the environment, and its economic context.

Investors are becoming more aware of the world's pressing social and environmental challenges, such as climate change, poverty, and inequality. They seek to invest in solutions to address these challenges and create a more sustainable future. Environmental, social, and governance (ESG) investing is becoming increasingly popular, and investors are increasingly demanding investments considering ESG factors. SII is a natural extension of ESG investing, as it explicitly focuses on generating positive social and environmental impact.

There is a growing movement to develop standardised metrics for measuring and reporting on social and environmental impact. This makes it easier for investors to assess the impact of their investments and make informed decisions.

Businesses should clearly articulate their social and environmental goals and objectives. This will help them identify potential impact investors aligned with their mission. They should regularly measure and report on their social and environmental impact. This will demonstrate to impact investors that they are serious about creating a positive impact. Companies must be transparent about their business practices, including their supply chain, labour practices, and environmental impact. This will help build trust with impact investors.

Impact investments can generate financial returns alongside social and environmental impact. This makes them a compelling investment opportunity for investors looking to make a positive difference in the world without sacrificing their financial goals.

Impact investments are often less risky than traditional investments. Impact businesses are often more resilient to economic downturns as they address fundamental social and environmental needs.

Impact investments can generate positive social and environmental impacts. This can help to address some of the world's most pressing challenges and create a more sustainable future.

Examples of Social Impact Investments

- Microfinance: Microfinance institutions provide small loans to entrepreneurs in developing countries, helping them to start and grow their businesses.
- Renewable energy: Renewable energy companies are developing and deploying clean technologies like solar and wind power.
- Affordable housing: Affordable housing developers are building and managing affordable housing for low-income families.
- Education: Educational technology companies are developing innovative tools and platforms to improve access to quality education.
- Healthcare: Healthcare companies are developing and delivering affordable healthcare solutions to underserved communities.

Social impact investing is a powerful tool for addressing the world's most pressing challenges and creating a more sustainable future. Businesses can play a critical role in generating positive social and environmental impact by aligning themselves with impact investors.

5.5 Avoid Greenwashing

In the era of growing environmental consciousness, businesses are increasingly embracing sustainability initiatives and promoting their environmental credentials. However, the line between genuine commitment to impact and mere marketing hype can be blurred, leading to greenwashing. You want to incorporate ESG and SDGs in the presentation, yet you do not want to be accused of greenwashing.

Greenwashing occurs when businesses make misleading or exaggerated claims about their environmental practices to gain a competitive edge or attract environmentally conscious consumers. This deceptive practice undermines consumer trust and erodes the integrity of sustainability efforts.

Genuine commitment to impact, on the other hand, goes beyond superficial claims and gestures. It involves a deep-rooted understanding of the environmental impact of business operations and a proactive approach to reducing that impact. Businesses that genuinely care about sustainability integrate environmental considerations into their decision-making processes, continuously strive for improvement, and transparently communicate their progress.

Businesses should be open and honest about their environmental practices, strengths, and weaknesses. They should provide clear and verifiable information about their sustainability efforts, such as emissions data and waste reduction targets.

Instead of making vague or exaggerated claims, businesses should focus on demonstrating their actual environmental impact. This can be done through quantifiable metrics, such as reductions in greenhouse gas emissions, water usage, or waste generation.

Obtaining certifications from reputable organisations provides independent validation of a company's sustainability claims.

Businesses should educate consumers about their environmental efforts and the importance of sustainability. This can be done through clear and concise communication, educational campaigns, and engagement with stakeholders.

Sustainability is an ongoing journey, not a destination. Businesses should commit to continuous improvement, regularly reviewing their environmental performance and setting ambitious goals for further reduction of their environmental footprint.

Businesses should avoid using vague or misleading terminology, such as "eco-friendly" or "sustainable," without providing concrete evidence to support these claims.

Businesses should extend their sustainability efforts to their supply chain, ensuring that their suppliers adhere to responsible environmental practices.

Marketing should accurately reflect the company's genuine sustainability efforts, avoiding exaggerated claims or creating unrealistic expectations.

Businesses should actively engage with stakeholders, including employees, customers, and environmental organisations, to seek feedback and incorporate their insights into their sustainability initiatives.

Regularly measure and report on environmental performance, providing transparent and accessible information to stakeholders.

By adopting these strategies, businesses can demonstrate their genuine commitment to impact, build trust with consumers, and contribute to a more sustainable future. Greenwashing is a disservice to sustainability efforts and can undermine public trust in business. Businesses that genuinely care about the environment should prioritise transparency, accountability, and measurable impact to maintain credibility and make a real difference.

Chapter 6 Navigating Regulatory Waters

6.1 Regulatory Environment

Raising capital is critical for private companies to grow and succeed. However, the regulatory environment governing capital raising varies from region to region. Private companies must understand the regulatory landscape in the regions where they seek to raise capital. You must take legal advice. The rules and regulations surrounding capital raising can vary significantly from one region to another, making it essential to understand the specific requirements in each location clearly.

Securities laws regulate securities issuance, sale, and trading, including stocks, bonds, and other investment instruments. Companies must comply with securities laws to raise capital from investors, and there are different sets of securities laws in different jurisdictions.

Tips for complying with capital raising regulations

- *Seek early guidance:* Engage with legal and financial professionals early in the capital raising process to understand the applicable regulations and plan accordingly. With the right knowledge, you can create a solid plan, ensuring compliance from the outset.

- *Stay informed about updates:* Regulatory environments are dynamic, so it's crucial to stay updated on any changes or amendments to capital raising regulations in your operating regions. Establish a system to monitor regulatory updates in the regions where you operate. Be prepared to adapt your capital raising strategy and documents to comply with the latest requirements.

- *Transparency and disclosure:* Maintain transparency and provide accurate disclosures to investors throughout the capital raising process. Maintain open and honest communication with potential investors, providing them with accurate and complete information about your company, its financial status, and the risks involved. Prepare comprehensive disclosure documents that outline all material information about your business and the investment opportunity. This fosters trust and helps avoid potential legal challenges.

- *Documentation and record-keeping:* Maintain comprehensive documentation and records related to capital raising activities, including investor communications, offering materials, and financial statements. Keep meticulous records of all investor communications, including emails, meetings, and phone calls. Maintain detailed records of all offering materials, such as prospectuses or private placement memorandums. Ensure your financial statements are up-to-date, accurate, and compliant with accounting standards.

6.2 Compliance Best Practices

Private companies must comply with various regulations, developing a compliance program when raising capital, including securities laws, anti-money laundering laws, and know-your-customer (KYC) laws. Compliance is important for many reasons. First, compliance can help private companies avoid costly regulatory fines and penalties. Second, compliance can help private companies to maintain their reputation and credibility with investors and other stakeholders. Third, compliance can help private companies to protect their investors from fraud and other financial risks.

There are best practices that private companies can follow to ensure compliance with regulatory requirements when raising capital.

The first step is developing a compliance program tailored to the company's needs. The compliance program should identify the company's risks and outline the steps that the company will take to mitigate those risks.

Private companies should conduct due diligence on all potential investors to ensure they are not investing in illegal or fraudulent activities. Private companies should also screen investors for sanctions and other financial risks.

Private companies must provide accurate and complete disclosure documents to potential investors. Disclosure documents should include information about the company's business model, financial performance, and risk factors.

Companies must also implement anti-money laundering and KYC procedures to prevent money laundering and terrorist financing. AML/KYC procedures should include verifying the identity of investors and monitoring transactions for suspicious activity.

Businesses must train their employees on their compliance policies and procedures. Employees should know the company's risks and their role in mitigating them.

Private companies must monitor their compliance with regulatory requirements on an ongoing basis. This includes reviewing their compliance program, conducting due diligence on investors, and updating their disclosure documents.

Common compliance mistakes

- Failing to develop a compliance program.
- Failing to conduct due diligence on investors.
- Failing to prepare accurate and complete disclosure documents.
- Failing to implement AML/KYC procedures.
- Failing to train employees on compliance policies and procedures.
- Failing to monitor compliance with regulatory requirements.

How to avoid compliance mistakes

Private companies should consult with an experienced securities lawyer to ensure they comply with all applicable regulations. There are templates and checklists online that can help private companies comply with regulatory requirements. A compliance management system can help private companies to automate and streamline their compliance process.

There are many professional certifications available for compliance professionals. A professional certification can demonstrate to regulators that the company is committed to compliance.

Compliance is essential for private companies that are raising capital. By following the best practices outlined above, private companies can reduce their risk of violating regulatory requirements and protect their investors from fraud and other financial risks.

The CEO must understand the importance of compliance and be committed to creating a culture of compliance within the company. The compliance program should be tailored to the specific needs of the company. The CEO should have access to experienced compliance professionals who can guide on specific compliance issues.

6.3 Disclaimers in Marketing Material

You need disclaimers on presentations when raising capital for private companies from investors. Disclaimers help to protect the company and its founders from legal liability. There are different types of disclaimers you may want to include in your presentation.

Forward-looking statements disclaimer: This disclaimer warns investors that the presentation contains forward-looking statements, which are statements about future events or conditions that are inherently uncertain. This disclaimer helps to protect the company from liability if the forward-looking statements do not come to pass.

Investment risk disclaimer: This disclaimer warns investors that investing in the company is risky. This helps to protect the company from liability if investors lose money on their investments.

No offer to sell disclaimer: This disclaimer warns investors that the presentation is not an offer to sell securities. This is important because it prevents investors from suing the company if they believe the presentation misled them.

In addition to these general disclaimers, you may also want to include specific disclaimers about your company's business, financial condition, or investment terms. For example, if your company is in a highly regulated industry, you may want to include a disclaimer about your business's regulatory risks.

Have a lawyer review your presentation before you deliver it to investors. A lawyer can help you to ensure that you have included all of the necessary disclaimers and that your presentation is otherwise compliant with the law.

Disclaimer example

This presentation contains forward-looking statements, which are statements about future events or conditions that are inherently uncertain. Actual results may differ materially from those expressed in these forward-looking statements. Forward-looking statements are based on assumptions about the company's business strategy, market conditions, and future financial performance. These assumptions are inherently uncertain and may not come to pass. Investors are cautioned not to place undue reliance on forward-looking statements.

Investing in the company is a risky investment. Investors could lose all or part of their investment. Investors should consider their investment objectives, risk tolerance, and financial condition before investing in the company.

This presentation is not an offer to sell securities. No offer to sell securities will be made unless and until a registration statement is filed with and declared effective by the Securities and Exchange Commission.

You can help protect your company and its founders from legal liability by including disclaimers in your presentation.

6.4 Privacy and Data Protection

In today's data-driven world, privacy and data protection are paramount concerns, especially when raising capital and handling investors' personal information. Regulations like the General Data Protection Regulation (GDPR) have been implemented to safeguard individuals' personal data, and companies involved in capital raising must adhere to these requirements.

The GDPR mandates that companies adopt appropriate measures to protect investors' data and ensure transparency in how their information is collected, processed, and stored. This includes obtaining clear and informed consent from investors before collecting their data, providing them access to their data upon request, and implementing robust data security measures to prevent unauthorised access or breaches.

Non-compliance with privacy regulations can lead to hefty fines and reputational damage. Compliance with privacy regulations goes beyond legal obligations; it is also an ethical responsibility. Respecting investors' privacy and treating their personal information carefully demonstrates a company's commitment to ethical practices and fosters long-term trust.

To ensure compliance and effectively manage investor data, companies should implement comprehensive data protection strategies.

Establish clear and comprehensive data protection policies that outline the company's approach to collecting, processing, storing, and disposing of investor data. Include your policy on your website.

Conduct regular audits and assessments to identify and address potential data privacy risks or vulnerabilities.

Implement robust data security measures, including encryption, access controls, and regular system updates, to safeguard investor data from unauthorised access or breaches.

Provide clear and accessible information to investors about how their personal data is collected, used, and shared. Obtain their informed consent before processing their data and allow them to access, correct, or delete their data upon request.

Here are some other examples of GDPR violations

Collecting personal data without consent: One of the key principles of the GDPR is that personal data can only be collected and processed if the individual has given their consent. This means that companies must have a clear and transparent privacy policy that explains how they collect and use personal data. They must obtain individuals' consent before collecting their data.

- *Failing to secure personal data:* Companies have a responsibility to take appropriate technical and organisational measures to protect personal data from unauthorised access, use, disclosure, alteration, or destruction. Companies must have robust data security systems and train their staff to protect personal data.
- *Failing to provide individuals with access to their data:* Individuals have the right to access their personal data and know how it is used. This means that companies must provide individuals with a copy of their data upon request, and they must explain how they are using the data.
- *Failing to delete personal data when requested:* Individuals have the right to delete their personal data in certain circumstances, such as if it is no longer necessary for the purpose for which it was collected. Companies must comply with these requests to delete personal data.
- *Failing to report data breaches:* Companies must report any breaches to the relevant supervisory authority within 72 hours of becoming aware of the breach. This includes breaches that affect the personal data of individuals in the EU, even if the company is not based in the EU.
- *Using personal data for purposes other than those for which it was collected*: Companies can only use personal data for the purposes for which it was collected unless the individual

has given their consent for the data to be used for other purposes.

- *Failing to keep personal data accurate and up-to-date:* Companies must take reasonable steps to ensure that personal data is accurate and up-to-date.
- *Failing to restrict the processing of personal data:* Companies can only process personal data if one of the legal bases for processing applies. This means that companies must have a valid reason for processing personal data and only process the data necessary for that purpose.
- *Failing to transfer personal data securely:* Companies must transfer personal data to countries outside the EU only if the country has adequate data protection.
- *Failing to appoint a data protection officer (DPO):* Companies that meet specific criteria must appoint a DPO. The DPO is responsible for ensuring that the company complies with the GDPR.

Case Study: Adaptation of XYZ Fintech Group to GDPR Compliance

XYZ Fintech Group, a European fintech company specialising in investment management, faced the challenge of adapting its processes to comply with the General Data Protection Regulation (GDPR). With a diverse investor base, the company managed a substantial amount of sensitive personal data.

Before the implementation of GDPR, XYZ Fintech Group's data handling processes were less structured, with data being stored in multiple systems without stringent access controls. The company's privacy policies were also not comprehensive, leading to potential risks in data management and protection.

To align with GDPR, XYZ Fintech Group undertook a comprehensive overhaul of its data handling and privacy protocols.

- *Data Audit and Mapping:* The company conducted a thorough audit to map out all the personal data it held, identifying what was collected, how it was processed, and who had access to it.
- *Updating Privacy Policies:* XYZ Fintech Group updated its privacy policies to make them more transparent and user-friendly, ensuring clear communication about data usage, storage, and the rights of the data subjects.
- *Data Minimisation and Purpose Limitation:* The company implemented strict data minimisation principles, ensuring that only necessary data for specific, lawful purposes was collected and processed.
- *Enhanced Data Security Measures:* XYZ Fintech Group invested in state-of-the-art encryption and cybersecurity measures to protect data from unauthorised access and breaches. Regular security audits were instituted to maintain high data security standards.
- *Employee Training and Awareness:* Comprehensive training programs were introduced to educate employees on GDPR requirements, data protection best practices, and the importance of maintaining data privacy.
- *Data Protection Officer (DPO) Appointment:* A DPO was appointed to oversee compliance efforts, handle data protection queries, and liaise with regulatory authorities.

XYZ Fintech Group experienced several significant benefits from its GDPR compliance efforts:

- *Enhanced Trust and Reputation:* Demonstrating a commitment to data protection significantly improved XYZ Fintech Group's reputation among investors, enhancing trust and confidence in the company.
- *Operational Efficiency:* The structured approach to data management led to more streamlined and efficient operations, with improved data quality and accessibility.
- *Risk Mitigation:* Compliance significantly reduced the risk of data breaches and the associated legal and financial consequences.
- *Competitive Advantage:* By adhering to high data protection standards, XYZ Fintech Group positioned itself as a leader in data privacy, attracting investors who valued stringent data security measures.

XYZ Fintech Group's journey to GDPR compliance exemplifies how adapting to privacy regulations is not only a legal requirement but can also bring operational and reputational benefits. The company's proactive stance in data protection set a standard in the fintech industry, reinforcing that effective data management and privacy protection are integral to business success and customer trust.

6.5 Know Your Customer and Anti-Money Laundering

Know Your Customer (KYC) and Anti-Money Laundering (AML) are key terms. Businesses must implement these essential processes to comply with regulatory requirements and prevent financial crimes.

Know Your Customer (KYC)

KYC is a process of verifying the identity of customers and assessing their potential risks. This process helps businesses ensure they are not onboarding or transacting with criminals or terrorist organisations.

Financial institutions and fintech companies must be aware of and comply with sanctions and embargoes imposed by various governments and international organisations. This includes screening transactions, customers, and counterparties against sanctions lists and implementing appropriate controls to prevent prohibited activities.

Key elements of KYC include:

- Collecting customer information: This includes verifying the customer's name, address, date of birth, and other relevant details.
- Document verification: This involves checking the authenticity of identity documents, such as passports, driver's licenses, and utility bills.
- Risk assessment: This involves evaluating the customer's financial behaviour, source of funds, and potential for involvement in illegal activities.

Anti-Money Laundering (AML)

AML is a set of measures that financial institutions and businesses must take to prevent money laundering. Money laundering is the process of converting illegally obtained money into seemingly legitimate funds.

Key elements of AML include:

- Transaction monitoring: This involves monitoring customer transactions for suspicious activity, such as large or unusual transactions.
- Reporting suspicious activity: Businesses must report suspicious transactions to regulatory authorities.
- Training employees: Employees must be trained to identify and report suspicious activity.

Importance of KYC and AML

They help prevent financial crimes: KYC and AML procedures help to identify and prevent criminals from using financial institutions to launder money or finance terrorist activities.

They protect businesses from legal and financial risks: Businesses that fail to comply with KYC and AML regulations can face significant fines, penalties, and reputational damage.

They promote transparency and trust: KYC and AML procedures help build trust in the financial system by ensuring businesses operate responsibly and ethically.

Case Study: Compliance Breach by Tam Tech

Tam Tech, a mid-sized software company, was poised for rapid expansion and sought to raise capital through private investments. With a promising portfolio of innovative products, the company attracted substantial interest from various investors. In its haste to secure funding, Tam Tech overlooked critical aspects of securities laws and AML/KYC regulations. The company failed to vet its investors properly, skipping essential due diligence processes. Moreover, in its investment presentations, Tam Tech made overly optimistic projections without adequate disclaimers, violating securities law requirements for transparent and balanced disclosure.

The irregularities came to light when a routine audit by financial regulators revealed discrepancies in investor profiles and questioned the accuracy of the company's financial disclosures.

Subsequently, Tam Tech faced legal action for:

- Non-compliance with Securities Laws: Misrepresentation in investment materials and failure to provide balanced financial projections.
- Violation of AML/KYC Regulations: Inadequate verification and screening of investors, leading to the accidental involvement of individuals linked to prohibited activities.

Tam Tech was subjected to:

- Fines and Penalties: The company was fined heavily for non-compliance with regulatory standards. These fines significantly impacted its financial standing.
- Mandatory Compliance Reforms: The company was ordered to overhaul its compliance program, incorporating stringent AML/KYC processes and ensuring adherence to securities laws.

The total cost of fines and legal fees amounted to a substantial portion of Tam Tech's capital reserves. Additionally, the cost of implementing new compliance measures and disrupting normal business activities added to the financial strain.

The legal action against Tam Tech received considerable media attention, casting a shadow over the company's credibility. Investor confidence plummeted, and several potential deals were lost. The damage to the company's reputation was exacerbated by public scrutiny and negative investor sentiment.

This case underscores the critical need for strict adherence to regulatory requirements in capital raising activities. Rigorous investor vetting is essential to prevent compliance breaches. Ensuring transparent and balanced information in investment materials is non-negotiable. Companies must adopt a proactive approach to compliance, regularly updating their practices to align with current laws and regulations.

Tam Tech's experience is a cautionary tale for other companies in the private capital raising arena. It highlights the importance of a robust compliance framework to satisfy regulatory requirements and maintain investor trust and corporate integrity. A company's long-term success in raising capital is significantly influenced by its commitment to compliance and ethical business practices.

6.6 Politically Exposed Persons (PEPs)

When raising capital, be aware of Politically Exposed Persons (PEPs) and their potential risks. PEPs hold prominent public positions that may increase their exposure to bribery, corruption, and money laundering. Due to their elevated risk profile, financial institutions and investors are subject to heightened scrutiny when dealing with PEPs.

Examples of PEPs include but are not limited to

• Heads of State or Government: Presidents, Prime Ministers, or leaders of other forms of government.

- Senior Politicians: Senior members of political parties, such as party leaders or high-ranking officials in governmental bodies.
- Government Officials: High-level government executives, advisors, or administrators, particularly those in departments that handle large budgets or sensitive information.
- Judiciary Members: Members of higher courts, such as Supreme Court judges or other senior judiciary officials, who have significant influence over legal and judicial matters.
- Senior Executives of State-Owned Corporations: CEOs, board members, or other high-ranking officials in state-owned enterprises, especially in industries like oil, gas, mining, and defence.
- Senior Military Officials: High-ranking military personnel, such as generals or admirals, significantly influence military and defence policy.
- Diplomats: Ambassadors, consuls, or high-ranking officials in international embassies and consulates.
- International Organization Officials: Senior executives or representatives at major international organisations like the United Nations, NATO, the European Union, the World Bank, or the International Monetary Fund.
- Family Members and Close Associates of the Above: Spouses, children, parents, and close associates of PEPs are often included under this category due to the potential for the PEP to use them as proxies for illicit activities.
- Members of Royal Families: In countries with monarchies, members of royal families often hold significant political influence and are included as PEPs.

Why PEP risks matter in capital raising

- *Regulatory Compliance:* Financial institutions and investors must comply with Anti-Money Laundering (AML) and Counter-Terrorist Financing (CTF) regulations. These regulations mandate thorough due diligence on PEPs to identify and mitigate potential risks.
- *Reputational Damage:* Associating with PEPs involved in financial misconduct can severely damage the reputation of a company or investment fund. This reputational harm can lead to loss of investor confidence, regulatory sanctions, and difficulties in future capital raising efforts.
- *Legal Liabilities:* Engaging in transactions with PEPs without proper due diligence can expose financial institutions and investors to legal liabilities. This includes potential criminal charges, civil lawsuits, and regulatory fines.

How to address PEP risks in capital raising

- *Implement robust PEP screening procedures:* Implement a system to identify and flag potential PEPs among investors or potential partners. This may involve using specialised PEP screening databases or conducting thorough background checks.
- *Conduct enhanced due diligence on PEPs*: For identified PEPs, conduct more in-depth due diligence to assess their risk profile. This may involve reviewing their financial history, political affiliations, and any previous involvement in financial misconduct.
- *Consider risk mitigation measures:* Implement appropriate measures based on the assessed risk level. This may include obtaining additional documentation, ongoing monitoring, or applying stricter transaction controls.

- *Stay informed and updated:* Keep abreast of changes in PEP regulations and industry best practices. Regularly review and update your PEP risk management procedures to ensure they remain effective.

6.7 Anti-Bribery Legislation

In the dynamic world of business, capital raising plays a pivotal role in fuelling growth, expanding operations, and achieving strategic goals. For private companies seeking to elevate their trajectory, securing funding from investors is often a crucial step. However, capital raising can be fraught with potential pitfalls, including the risk of bribery and corruption. Bribery, the offering or acceptance of an improper inducement to influence behaviour, can have devastating consequences for individuals and organisations.

The global fight against bribery and corruption has gained momentum over the past few decades, leading to the development of a robust framework of anti-bribery legislation. These laws, enacted at national and international levels, aim to deter and punish bribery practices that undermine fair competition and economic growth.

One of the most prominent anti-bribery laws is the United States Foreign Corrupt Practices Act (FCPA), which prohibits U.S. companies and their representatives from bribing foreign officials to obtain or retain business. Similarly, the UK Bribery Act criminalises bribery of both foreign and domestic officials and bribery committed by individuals acting on behalf of companies.

At the international level, the Organisation for Economic Co-operation and Development (OECD) Anti-Bribery Convention serves as a cornerstone of global efforts to combat bribery. The Convention outlines a comprehensive set of principles and standards that signatory countries are committed to implementing in their domestic laws.

A key distinction exists between civil and criminal liability for bribery offences. Civil liability generally involves financial penalties and damages, while criminal liability can lead to imprisonment and fines. The specific legal consequences vary depending on the jurisdiction and the severity of the offence.

The consequences of bribery in capital raising extend far beyond the immediate financial transaction. Bribery can severely damage a company's reputation, eroding investor trust and tarnishing its brand image. This reputational damage can make it difficult to attract future capital, hindering the company's growth prospects.

Furthermore, bribery can lead to a tangled web of legal complications. Both individuals and organisations can face severe legal repercussions, including criminal charges, fines, and regulatory sanctions. These legal consequences can have a crippling effect on a company's operations, jeopardising its financial stability and even its survival.

The capital raising process, from identifying potential investors to closing the deal, presents several stages where bribery risks can arise. Understanding these risks is crucial for developing effective mitigation strategies.

1. *Identifying Potential Investors:* The initial stage of identifying and screening potential investors is a critical entry point for bribery risks. Intermediaries or third-party agents may attempt to influence investment decisions through bribes, seeking to gain favour for their clients or secure personal benefits.

2. *Due Diligence:* Companies assess potential investors' financial health and suitability during the due diligence phase. This process involves examining financial statements,

verifying identities, and evaluating potential conflicts of interest. Bribery can occur if companies overlook red flags or fail to conduct thorough background checks.

3. *Negotiating Investment Terms:* The negotiation stage involves determining the terms of the investment, including the amount of capital provided, ownership stakes, and profit-sharing agreements. Bribery risks arise when individuals seek to influence these negotiations in their favour, potentially compromising the company's interests.

4. *Closing the Deal:* The final stage involves finalising legal agreements, transferring funds, and securing regulatory approvals. Bribery can occur during this stage if individuals seek to expedite approvals, secure favourable terms, or avoid scrutiny.

Educating employees about anti-bribery laws and company policies is crucial for preventing and detecting bribery. Regular training sessions and ongoing awareness campaigns help employees understand their responsibilities and identify potential risks.

Develop a comprehensive training program covering relevant laws, company policies, and procedures. This training should be tailored to employees' roles and responsibilities in capital raising activities. Provide ongoing training and updates to employees to inform them of the latest anti-bribery legislation and company policy developments. This ongoing education ensures that employees can address emerging risks and uphold ethical standards.

Chapter 7 Placement Agents and Introducers

7.1 Benefits of External Advisors

TPMs are crucial in connecting companies with potential investors. Using placement agents or introducers, also referred to as third-party marketers (TPM), can be a helpful way for CEOs to raise capital.

These professionals have a deep network of contacts with potential investors and can help CEOs navigate the capital raising process. They have seen it all before and can help you mentally prepare for the journey.

- *Access to a broader pool of investors.* TPMs can access a wider pool of investors than CEOs. This can be especially helpful for early-stage companies or companies raising capital in a new industry.
- *Expertise in the capital raising process.* TPMs have experience helping companies to raise capital. They can help CEOs develop a capital raising strategy, prepare pitch materials, reach out to investors and set up meetings, organise dry runs, and negotiate with investors. Most CEOs are not aware of what they do not know.
- *Time savings.* TPMs can save CEOs a lot of time by handling the outreach and logistics of the capital raising process. This allows CEOs to focus on running their businesses.

7.2 Typical Compensation

- *Retainer fee:* A retainer fee is a monthly or quarterly payment that the TPM receives from the client, regardless of whether they successfully raise capital. Retainer fees typically range from $5,000 to $20,000 per month, payable up to six months on average. Some may work without a retainer, but you cannot expect commitment by only paying a success fee. You may hear from them or never hear from them, as they will always prioritise their retained clients.

- *Success fee:* A performance fee is a percentage of the capital the TPM helps raise for the client. It is charged on initial and all follow-on investments by investors. Performance fees typically range from 5% to 10% of the total capital raised, depending on the size and perceived difficulty of the capital raise. They may receive a success bonus if they can raise a certain amount of capital for the client. For amounts higher than GBP30 million, the percentage for success fees may start to trail down.

- In addition to the retainer and success fees, TPMs may also receive additional compensation, such as travel expenses or options in the business.

In the initial capital raising round, a TPM raises $10 million for a private company round. The TPM charges a 5% commission, so they receive $500,000. The private company then raises an additional $20 million in follow-on investments. The TPM continues to provide value to the client during the follow-on investments if the initial investor invests more. As a result, the TPM receives an additional 5% commission on the follow-on investments, which is $1 million.

The specific terms of compensation for a TPM will vary depending on the size and stage of the company, the experience of the TPM, and the complexity of the capital raising campaign. The TPM and the client need to understand the terms of compensation before entering a contract.

Additional terms that may be requested

- *Exclusivity*: Some TPMs may require exclusivity, meaning they are the only TPM the client can work with. This can be good if the TPM is experienced and has a strong track record. However, ensuring that the exclusivity agreement is fair and that the client has an easy way to terminate the contract if they are not satisfied with the TPM's performance is essential. Of course, any introduction made before termination should be honoured, and success fees will be due.
- *Timeline:* Agree on a timeline for the capital raising campaign. This will help to ensure that both the TPM and the client are aligned on expectations. However, a TPM cannot control the closing of the transaction, only the timing of introductions. Many delays often are caused by the company.
- *Communication:* Establish clear communication channels with the TPM. This will help to ensure that both parties are kept informed of the progress of the capital raising campaign.

When you contract with a big firm, your first contact person may be one of the partners, but the execution could be done by a junior who joined yesterday. Ask who will be executing and reaching out to investors on your behalf. Use a TPM who is a good fit for your company. Not all TPMs are created equal.

Finding a TPM you like who has experience in your industry and understands your company's development and needs is important. You may be spending a lot of time with a TPM on planes so make sure you get along.

7.3 Reasons for Rejecting Your Company

TPMs do not say yes to every company that knocks on their door. They have limited bandwidth and will meticulously evaluate potential clients to ensure they are working with companies that have the highest probability of a successful fundraising process. They will want to make sure they protect their reputation. An overview of some of the criteria TPMs consider when deciding whether to take on a new client:

Before an introductory call

- **Bandwidth:** TPMs assess their current workload to determine if they can handle additional mandates. They may decline the opportunity without further consideration if their schedule is already full.
- **Convincing Pitch:** TPMs scrutinise the clarity and persuasiveness of the company's proposal. Thorough and consistent documentation demonstrates a professional and transparent approach, increasing the likelihood of securing an investment.
- **Investor, Sector and Geographical fit:** TPMs carefully consider whether the proposed investment aligns with their existing investor base's risk appetite and preferences. They are more inclined to accept mandates that match their investors' interests. TPMs often specialise in specific industries or sectors. If a company's business falls outside its

area of expertise, they may decline to pursue the mandate. TPMs may have a geographical focus, either domestically or internationally. If a company's target market is outside of their geographical scope, they may not be able to effectively connect them with potential investors. So, if you receive a rejection, it does not mean your proposal is not good, but it may not be a fit with the expertise of the TPM.

After an introductory call

- **Management Team's Expertise and Track Record:** TPMs evaluate the management team's capabilities to execute the business plan and successfully close a deal. They seek experienced entrepreneurs with a proven track record of success. High turnover within the management team is a red flag. Frequent changes in the client's team, strategy, or business model may indicate instability or an inability to execute a consistent long-term plan.
- **Regulatory, Compliance, or Legal Issues:** TPMs are hesitant to work with companies with a history of regulatory, compliance, or legal issues. Such issues could expose their firm to reputational risks. Any issues they may find googling the company or the management team may be a reason for passing.
- **Does the Company have an Edge?** TPMs assess the size and potential of the market in which the company operates. Does the company solve a real, immediate and common problem? A large and growing market with clear differentiation is more attractive to investors. TPMs evaluate the company's competitive position within the industry. A strong competitive advantage and defensible market position are key factors for success. TPMs consider the company's intellectual property portfolio, such as

patents, trademarks, or copyrights. Strong IP protection provides a competitive advantage and enhances investment value.

- **Due Diligence Cooperation:** TPMs expect full cooperation from potential clients during due diligence processes to assess their legitimacy and mitigate potential risks. Unwillingness to cooperate raises red flags. Companies asking for an NDA to be signed before even sending their deck will be a red flag indicating a lack of experience.

- **Adequate Capitalization:** TPMs assess whether the company has sufficient capital or an investor base with deep pockets to support its operations and fundraising efforts. Insufficient capital may lead to rejection. They will focus on the burn rate, which shows how quickly you spend your capital. This gives them an indication of how much time there is to raise the capital. If there is insufficient runway, they will shy away from the mandate.

- **Existing Investor Base:** TPMs are more comfortable taking on the mandate if the company has reputable institutional investors on board. They view institutional investors as a sign of credibility and professionalism that will help them to execute.

- **Realistic Time Frame:** Raising capital can be a time-consuming process. Clients may have unrealistic expectations about the speed at which funds can be raised, leading to frustration. Unrealistic expectations may discourage them from taking on the mandate. Anyone who talks about a three-month capital raising process will likely face rejection.

- **Commercials and Negotiations:** TPMs expect fair and transparent compensation for their services. Unclear or unappealing terms may lead to rejection. One-sided negotiations are also a major red flag.

- **Preference for Exclusivity:** If the company already has another TPM working on the deal, it may be a reason for passing. If multiple TPMs work on the same deal, creating competition, it potentially reduces the chances of success for each agent involved. They will prefer to work for a client who gives them an exclusive for at least the first three months. You risk no one prioritising your capital raise as they hedge their time invested. If another investor is in due diligence, they may pass as they feel their efforts are used to introduce competition to edge that investor along.

- **Payment History:** Late or non-payment of fees by clients can be a significant concern for TPMs. Ensuring that clients fulfil their financial obligations is essential for sustaining their business. TPMs review the company's payment history to ensure a good track record of paying on time. A history of late payments or bad treatment of previous TPMs raises concerns.

By carefully considering these criteria, TPMs make informed decisions about which mandates to pursue, ensuring successful capital raising and protecting their reputation in the industry.

7.4 Who to Hire: Selection Criteria

Before hiring a TPM or introducer, be sure to do your research and interview multiple candidates. Get references from other CEOs who have used the TPM's services. It would help if you liked them as you will spend considerable time on the road together. TPMs typically charge a percentage-based fee. They may also charge retainers. Be sure to negotiate the fee before signing any contracts, yet ensure your TPM is motivated. They will unlikely go the extra mile if they are unhappy with your counter-proposal. Be sure to get all your agreements with the TPM or introducer in writing. This will help to protect you in case of any disputes. After hiring a TPM, closely monitor the capital raising process. Ask questions and ensure you are comfortable with the investors and investment terms being presented to you.

Ten traits a third-party capital raiser needs to have

1. *Strong track record:* A proven track record of success in raising capital is essential for any third-party capital raiser. There is, however, no guarantee that they will be able to do the same for you, as each fundraiser is different.
2. *Deep industry knowledge:* A deep understanding of the industry or sector in which the company operates is crucial for a third-party capital raiser. This allows them to effectively identify and target potential investors and position the company to the right audience. This is a plus if they recently did a similar mandate, as they will already have a short list of potential investors.
3. *Extensive network of contacts:* A third-party capital raiser should have a strong network of contacts in the investment community, including institutional investors, private equity firms, and venture capitalists. This network will be invaluable in sourcing potential investors and connecting the company with the right capital partners.
4. *Exceptional communication and presentation skills:* Effective communication and presentation skills are essential for any TPM. They need to articulate the company's investment proposition, generate excitement and enthusiasm among potential investors, and handle investor inquiries and due diligence requests professionally, confidently, clearly, and concisely.
5. *Ability to build relationships:* Building strong relationships

with potential investors is critical for successful capital raising. A TPM should be able to cultivate trust, rapport, and mutual understanding with investors, fostering long-term relationships that can lead to repeat business and referrals.

6. *Negotiation and deal structuring expertise:* Skilled negotiation and deal structuring abilities are helpful for a TPM. They need to be able to negotiate favourable terms for the company while ensuring that the investment structure aligns with the interests of both the company and the investors. Some companies prefer to do the negotiations themselves and only use TPMs to arrange meetings.

7. *Financial literacy:* A solid understanding of financial modelling and valuation is a plus for a TPM. They must be able to assess the company's valuation and financial projections and communicate its financial performance effectively to potential investors.

8. *Strong market intelligence and due diligence skills:* Staying current on market trends, competitor analysis, and regulatory changes is crucial for a TPM. They need to be able to conduct thorough due diligence on potential investors and ensure that the company is making informed decisions about its capital partners.

9. *High integrity and ethics:* A TPM must have the highest integrity and ethical standards. They should be transparent in their dealings with the company and potential investors, upholding the trust that has been placed in them.

10. *Ability to work independently and as part of a team:* A TPM should take the initiative and collaborate effectively with the company's management team and other advisors. They should be able to manage multiple projects concurrently and keep stakeholders informed throughout the capital raising process.

Traits you do not want your TPM to have

1. *Lack of transparency:* A TPM who is not transparent about their fees, the capital raising process, or potential risks to the investment is a red flag. You should be able to trust your capital raiser to be upfront and honest with you about all aspects of the deal and any introductions being made.
2. *Unrealistic expectations:* A TPM who promises to raise more money or at a higher valuation than is realistic sets you up for failure. Be wary of TPMs who make promises that sound too good. They may promise they can raise the money in three months because that is what you want to hear.
3. *Conflict of interest:* A TPM with a conflict of interest, such as financial ties to a competing company, should be avoided. You want to ensure that your TPM acts in your best interests, not theirs.
4. *Poor communication skills:* A TPM who cannot communicate effectively with you, potential investors, and other stakeholders can be a major liability. You need to be able to rely on your capital raiser to keep you informed and updated throughout the capital raising process.
5. *Lack of experience:* A TPM who lacks experience in your industry or with companies of your size and stage of development may not be the best choice for you. You want to work with someone with a proven track record of success in raising capital for companies like yours.
6. *Unprofessional conduct:* A TPM who exhibits unprofessional behaviour, such as being late for meetings, not returning calls or emails, or making disparaging remarks about your company or competitors, should be dismissed. You want to work with someone professional and respectful of your time and business.

7. *Lack of follow-through:* A TPM who does not follow through on their commitments can be a major headache. You need to trust your capital raiser to do what they say they will do when they do it.

8. *Excessive fees:* Be sure to compare fees from different capital raisers before deciding. Going for the cheapest is not advisable either. TPMs offer different services, so assess what is on offer versus the fees.

9. *Poor reputation:* A TPM with a poor reputation in the industry should be avoided. You want to work with someone respected and with a good track record of success.

TPMs must fully understand your company's business, financials, and risks to market your business to potential investors. Be transparent about all aspects of your company, even the negative ones. Be realistic about your valuation. Companies often have unrealistic expectations about how much money they can raise and at what valuation.

Capital raising is a marathon, not a sprint. It takes time to build relationships with investors and close deals. Be patient and keep going even if you don't raise as much money as you hoped for in the first round. Be prepared to work hard and be available when the TPM needs you on a call or to answer investor questions not previously anticipated. Do not expect the TPM to do everything for you. TPMs cannot perform miracles. It is a team effort.

Above all, ensure your TPM is motivated and treat them well. They are dealing with rejections from investors every day. They need to think you are fantastic when selling your investment proposition.

It is a process, not an event. Companies must be prepared to spend months or even years developing their investor pitch, meeting with potential investors, and conducting due diligence.

7.5 Stereotypes Debunked

You do not need to be an extrovert in capital raising

The common stereotype that only extroverts are successful in capital raising is a misconception that numerous real-world experiences have debunked. While extroverts are often seen as natural salespeople due to their outgoing and friendly nature, introverts possess unique skills and qualities that can be equally, if not more, effective in sales. Being an introvert can be a powerful asset in raising capital.

- *The Power of Listening:* Introverts are typically excellent listeners. In sales, listening carefully to what a customer is saying is invaluable. It allows the salesperson to understand the customer's needs, problems, and preferences. This deep understanding enables introverts to tailor their sales approach to each customer, offering genuinely relevant and beneficial solutions. Good listening skills also help build trust and rapport, as customers feel heard and understood.
- *Building Deeper Relationships:* Introverts often excel at building deep and meaningful relationships. While they might not engage in small talk as easily as extroverts, they tend to create stronger connections once they do engage. In sales, this ability to form deeper relationships can lead to more loyal customers and long-term partnerships. Customers appreciate the genuine care and attention they receive, which goes a long way in fostering trust and loyalty.
- *Preparation and Thoughtfulness:* Introverts are generally more inclined towards preparation and thoughtful analysis. Before a sales meeting, an introvert will likely spend time preparing, researching the client, and planning their

approach. This preparation can make them more effective in their sales pitch, as they are well informed about the product and the customer's potential needs and objections. Their thoughtful approach to sales conversations makes them more likely to provide well-considered, relevant responses and solutions.

- *Focused Conversations:* Introverts prefer one-on-one or small group conversations, common in many sales scenarios. They are comfortable in settings where they can have focused, in-depth discussions, often more productive than larger, more superficial interactions. This preference aligns well with many sales interactions involving detailed discussions about products or services.

- *Embracing Technology:* The rise of digital communication has been a boon for introverts in sales. This allows introverts to communicate effectively in a less direct and overwhelming way. These tools enable them to carefully think through their messages and responses, ensuring clarity and effectiveness in their communication.

- *Quality Over Quantity:* While extroverts may excel in making many sales calls or contacts, introverts often focus on the quality of each interaction. This quality-over-quantity approach can be particularly effective in industries where the sales cycle is longer and more complex or where building trust is essential.

- *Harnessing Creativity:* Introverts are often very creative thinkers. They can bring innovative perspectives to solving customer problems and may develop unique sales strategies that set them apart from their competitors. This creativity can be a significant advantage in finding and capitalising on new sales opportunities.

- *Calm and Composed:* Introverts usually have a calm and composed demeanour, which can be very effective in navigating the high-pressure situations that sometimes arise in sales. Their ability to remain calm under pressure can help diffuse tense situations and reassure customers.

- *Learning and Development:* Introverts are often keen learners and constantly seek to improve their skills. In the context of sales, they will likely embrace training and development opportunities, continually enhancing their sales skills and knowledge.
- *Challenges and Overcoming Them:* Introverts face certain challenges in sales, such as networking and cold calling, which can be more natural for extroverts. However, introverts can overcome these challenges by leveraging their strengths and finding strategies that work for them. For example, they can focus on building strong relationships in smaller networking groups or use digital communication methods for initial contact.

In conclusion, while extroverts may naturally gravitate towards capital raising roles, introverts possess unique skills that can make them equally successful. The key is to recognise and harness these strengths. In today's diverse business environment, there is room for both extroverts and introverts to excel in sales. By understanding and valuing the different qualities each brings to the table, sales teams can become more versatile, effective, and successful.

Capital raisers are always pushy and aggressive

The traditional image of capital raisers as pushy and aggressive is far from what successful sales look like today. Modern sales strategies emphasise building trust and establishing long-term customer relationships. Sales professionals are now trained to be consultative, which means they act more as advisors than traditional salespeople. They focus on understanding the customer's unique challenges and needs and then suggest real value solutions. Empathy is a crucial skill in modern sales. Salespeople are encouraged to put themselves in their customer's shoes to genuinely understand and address their concerns. This approach fosters a more respectful and productive sales process.

Raising capital is all about smooth-talking

While communication skills are undeniably important in sales, the notion that raising capital is solely about being a smooth talker is misleading. Effective sales communication involves listening actively, understanding, and responding to customer needs and problems. Successful salespeople engage in meaningful conversations. They ask insightful questions that help uncover the customer's true needs, enabling them to offer tailored solutions. Clearly articulating product benefits and how they meet customer needs is more valued than just persuasive rhetoric. It's about making relevant connections between a customer's requirements and the offered solution.

Capital raisers will say anything to make a sale

Contrary to the stereotype that capital raisers are willing to make false promises to close a deal, integrity and honesty are fundamental in modern sales practices. Misleading customers may result in immediate sales but damage trust, reputation, and long-term relationships. Building trust with honesty and transparency leads to customer loyalty and satisfaction, which are key drivers of sustainable business growth. Sales professionals are trained to be honest about their products, including capabilities and limitations, ensuring customer expectations are met and maintained.

Success in capital raising is all about natural talent

While it is true that certain innate traits like sociability and assertiveness can be advantageous in sales, the idea that success in sales is solely based on natural talent is misleading. Like any other professional skill, sales skills can be learned, honed, and mastered over time. Training plays a crucial role in a capital raiser's development. Effective sales training programs cover a range of skills, including negotiation, prospecting, product knowledge, customer relationship management, and digital sales techniques. Experience is another critical factor. Over time, sales professionals learn to navigate different sales scenarios, understand diverse customer behaviours, and refine their approach accordingly.

A willingness to learn and adapt is perhaps one of the most important traits of a successful salesperson. The best salespeople continuously seek to improve their skills and adapt to changing market conditions and customer needs. Strategic thinking, planning, and execution are equally important in sales. Understanding market trends, aligning sales strategies with customer needs, and effectively managing a sales pipeline are skills developed through experience and dedication.

Chapter 8 Finding Investors

8.1 Where to Find New Investors

This chapter will cover finding potential investors. First, you need to determine who your audience is and what the right investors are. Understand your investors and decide what channels you will use to engage with your target audience. In addition to friends, family, ex-colleagues, and bosses, networking is among the best ways to find potential investors.

Attend industry events, meetups, and conferences to meet potential investors. Several online platforms, such as AngelList, Crunchbase, Pitchbook, and Fundable, can help CEOs find investors. Ask friends, family, and advisors for referrals to potential investors. Leverage alumni networks, such as university or business school alumni groups, which can be a valuable source of potential investors.

Conferences and industry events are a great way to network with potential investors, learn about their investment criteria, and pitch your business. Conferences can attract hundreds or even thousands of investors, allowing you to connect with people interested in investing in your business. Conferences often have pitch competitions or other events where you can pitch your business to potential investors. This is a great way to get your business in front of people actively looking for new investment opportunities. Conferences can be a great way to meet entrepreneurs and industry experts who can provide valuable advice and support.

Use Professional Networking Sites like LinkedIn. CEOs can use these platforms to connect with potential investors, join industry-specific groups, and participate in discussions to increase visibility and credibility.

Some organisations, like investment banks, third party marketers and placement agents, specialise in connecting startups with investors. These services can be particularly useful for finding investors who are actively looking for new investment opportunities in specific industries or at specific growth stages.

Legal and Accounting Firms also often have networks of investors and can make introductions. They also provide valuable advice on preparing for investment.

Participate in Startup Competitions and Accelerator Programs. Many of these programs offer opportunities to pitch directly to investors. They can also provide valuable feedback, mentorship, and networking opportunities.

Collaboration with Industry Associations and Chambers of Commerce. They often have networks of business professionals and investors. They may host networking events, workshops, and seminars where entrepreneurs can meet potential investors.

Online Startup Communities and Forums. Engaging in online communities where entrepreneurs and investors gather can be a useful way to gain insights, seek advice, and potentially connect with interested investors.

Build an online presence and use social media. Developing a strong online presence through a company website, blog, or social media can attract investors. Sharing insights, company updates, and industry news can help build credibility and visibility.

Gaining media coverage can increase a company's visibility to potential investors. This can include press releases, interviews, or articles in industry publications.

Sometimes, the direct approach can be effective. This involves identifying potential investors and reaching out to them with a tailored pitch or meeting request.

8.2 Investor Segmentation

Segmentation can include investment type, stage, industry focus, size, and geographic location. Segmentation helps companies identify the investor groups most likely to be interested in their investment opportunity.

This allows you to tailor their communication and outreach efforts to resonate with each segment's interests and preferences. Once the investor pool has been segmented, companies must prioritise and focus on the most relevant segments to their capital raising goals.

When targeting investor segments, factors include alignment with the company's stage and industry. Companies should target segments with the financial capacity to invest in their desired amount. Targeting investors with smaller investment capacity may not be aligned with the company's funding needs. Investors have varying risk tolerance levels and willingness to invest in early-stage or high-risk ventures. Companies should target segments that align with their risk profile and investment timeline.

8.3 Types of Investors

CEOs can go to various investors for funding, depending on the stage of their company and the type of investment they seek. There are different types of investors that CEOs can approach for funding: friends and family, angel investors, online crowdfunding platforms, accelerators and incubators, impact investors, venture capitalists, family offices, hedge funds, government agencies, private equity funds, insurance companies, pension funds, strategic investors and sovereign wealth funds.

Angel investors

Angel investors are individuals who invest their own money in early-stage companies. Angel investors typically invest smaller amounts of money than VCs, but they are often more willing to invest in companies at a very early stage of development. Angel investors are often motivated to invest in companies because they believe in the company's mission or are excited about its potential. Angel investors may also invest in companies to help entrepreneurs succeed.

Pitching to angel investors might be more personal and narrative-driven, focusing on the vision and potential impact of the company.

Online Investment Platforms

These platforms, also known as equity crowdfunding platforms, allow individuals to invest in early-stage companies in exchange for equity. They bridge the gap between investors and startups, making it easier for smaller investors to participate in venture funding.

Accelerators and Incubators

These organisations support early-stage, growth-driven companies through education, mentorship, and financing. Startups enter accelerators for a fixed period and as part of a cohort of companies. The accelerator experience is a process of intense, rapid, and immersive education aimed at accelerating the life cycle of young, innovative companies.

Impact Investors

These are investors who are focused on generating a measurable, beneficial social or environmental impact alongside a financial return. They are particularly relevant for social enterprises and businesses that are built around solving societal or environmental issues.

Venture Capitalists (VCs)

Venture capitalists are professional investors who invest in early-stage companies with high growth potential. VCs typically provide large amounts of funding, but they also expect a high return on their investment.

VCs are often attracted to companies developing new technologies, disrupting existing industries, or having a large addressable market. VCs also typically look for companies with solid management teams and a clear vision for the future.

To engage a venture capital firm, emphasise the potential for exponential growth and highlight the scalability of your business model. Showcase how your innovative solution solves a pressing problem in the market and why your team is uniquely qualified to execute the plan. Remember to emphasise the potential return on investment and how your venture fits into their portfolio strategy.

Family offices

Family offices are private investment firms that manage the wealth of wealthy families. They can invest in various assets, including stocks, bonds, and real estate. They do not have to invest like a VC or Private Equity Fund. They can stay on the sidelines. When pitching to a family office or more conservative investors, focus on stability, steady revenue growth, and risk mitigation strategies. Highlight your proven track record, customer base, and long-term profitability potential. Emphasise how your business aligns with their values and long-term investment goals.

Family offices value long-term relationships and are typically interested in preserving and growing their wealth over multiple generations. In your pitch, demonstrate that your business offers stability by showcasing consistent revenue growth and profitability. Highlight any risk mitigation strategies you have in place. Show how your business has a clear path to continued growth and sustainability, backed by a well-defined strategy, strong market positioning, and a solid competitive advantage.

Strategic investors

Strategic investors are companies that invest in other companies for strategic reasons. Pitch your investment, focusing on the strategic angle and potential for synergies. For example, a company may invest in a competitor to access its technology or enter a new market. A company may also invest in a supplier to secure its supply chain.

Strategic investors can provide several benefits to companies, including access to capital, expertise, and resources. However, it is crucial for CEOs to thoroughly evaluate potential strategic investors before accepting their investment offers. Understanding their motivations and ensuring alignment with your long-term vision is paramount. While financial benefits are important considerations when evaluating investment opportunities, maintaining control over the direction and core values of the company should also be carefully safeguarded. By carefully selecting partners who share your vision and goals while complementing your strengths as an organisation, you can set a solid foundation for future success.

Hedge funds

Hedge funds primarily focus on public markets and more liquid assets like stocks, bonds, currencies, and commodities. While some hedge funds may allocate a portion of their portfolio to private equity, venture capital, or private debt investments, it's not their primary area of expertise or focus.

While some hedge funds may diversify their portfolios by allocating a portion to private investments, they are not typically considered specialists in the private markets. Private equity firms and venture capital firms are the primary players in the private investment space, and they specialise in identifying, acquiring, and nurturing private companies.

It is important to note that the allocation of hedge fund assets to private investments can vary widely among different hedge funds, and the strategies employed by hedge funds can be quite diverse. However, the core focus of most hedge funds remains on public market investments and trading strategies.

Private equity firms

Private equity firms raise funds from various sources, including institutional investors like pension funds, endowments, and high-net-worth individuals. These funds are typically pooled into a private equity fund, and the PE firm then uses the capital to make investments. Private equity investments can take various forms, including leveraged buyouts (LBOs), venture capital, growth capital, and distressed asset acquisitions. The choice of investment type depends on the specific goals and strategies of the firm. Private equity firms often work closely with the management teams of their portfolio companies to implement operational improvements, cost-saving measures, and strategic initiatives. These efforts are aimed at increasing the company's profitability and value.

Private equity firms typically have a longer investment horizon compared to other investors, such as hedge funds. Their investment horizon can range from a few years to a decade or more. Private equity firms have various exit strategies to realise returns on their investments. Common exit options include selling the portfolio company to another company, conducting an initial public offering (IPO), or selling it to another private equity firm.

Pitching to private equity firms should be data-driven, emphasising financial performance, market position, and growth potential.

Pension funds

Pension funds are created to provide retirement benefits to employees or members of a pension plan. Their primary objective is to accumulate and manage assets that can generate income to meet future pension obligations.

Pension funds often engage in liability-driven investing (LDI) to match the returns of their investments with the timing and size of their future pension liabilities. This involves managing assets in a way that aligns with the expected payout schedule of pensions.

Pension funds have a long-term investment horizon since their obligations extend over many years or even decades. They need to balance the need for growth to meet future liabilities while preserving capital and managing risk.

Pension funds typically invest in a mix of asset classes, including stocks, bonds, real estate, and alternative investments, to achieve their long-term goals. They may also diversify globally to spread risk. Pension fund managers have a fiduciary duty to act in the best interests of plan participants and beneficiaries. This includes prudently managing investments and minimising conflicts of interest.

A pension fund will typically invest in larger, more established companies and are conservative investors. It is unlikely that a pension fund will invest in loss-making companies or startups.

Insurance companies

Insurance companies often invest in various types of assets, including private companies. These investments are part of their overall investment strategy to manage the funds collected from policyholders' premiums.

Insurance companies seek to diversify their investment portfolios to minimise risk. This diversification often includes investments in private companies, which can offer different risk and return profiles compared to public market investments. They might invest in private equity, which involves buying stakes in private companies. These investments are typically long-term and seek higher returns to compensate for the higher risk and illiquidity compared to publicly traded securities. Some insurance companies also invest in venture capital, focusing on startups and early-stage companies with high growth potential and will usually have a strategic angle for the business.

The returns sought by insurance companies from their investments in private companies can vary significantly. Given the higher risk and longer investment horizon, they generally look for higher returns from these types of investments compared to traditional fixed-income securities.

Since investments in private companies can be riskier and less liquid, insurance companies carefully manage the proportion of their total investment portfolio allocated to these investments. The strategies and risk tolerance can vary significantly between different insurance companies, depending on their size, type, and regulatory environment.

Government agencies

Government agencies play a crucial role in supporting small businesses by offering a range of loan and grant programs. Their mission is to help entrepreneurs and small business owners succeed. Such agencies provide loans with favourable terms and low interest rates, making it easier for small businesses to access the capital they need to start, expand, or recover from unforeseen challenges. These loans can be used for various purposes, including purchasing equipment, acquiring real estate, or refinancing existing debt.

In addition to loans, government agencies may offer grant programs that financially assist small businesses in specific industries or sectors. These grants can fund research and development projects, hire and train employees, or invest in innovative technologies. By leveraging the resources and expertise of government agencies, small businesses can access vital funding opportunities that may not be available through traditional lending channels. This support helps businesses thrive and contributes to job creation and economic growth. Take advantage of these resources and give your business the boost it needs to thrive in today's competitive landscape.

Sovereign wealth funds

Sovereign Wealth Funds (SWFs) invest in private companies. Their ticket sizes tend to be large, so they are generally not suitable if you are an early-stage company.

Like other large institutional investors, SWFs often seek to diversify their portfolios to optimise returns and manage risk. Private companies can offer higher returns than traditional investments like bonds or publicly traded stocks, albeit with higher risk.

SWFs may invest directly in private companies or through private equity funds. These investments can range from minority stakes to complete buyouts, depending on the fund's investment strategy and the target company's valuation and growth potential. Many SWFs are known for their long-term investment horizon.

Their investment strategies are typically driven by a combination of financial goals and the economic or strategic interests of their respective countries. As such, their involvement in private companies can have significant economic and sometimes geopolitical implications. They often make strategic investments in sectors that align with the economic objectives of their home country, such as technology, energy, infrastructure, or healthcare.

Approach different investors depending on your stage

The type of institutional investors that CEOs should approach will depend on the stage of their company and the type of investment they seek.

Early-stage companies should start by approaching friends and family, angel investors, accelerators and incubators, crowdfunding platforms and VCs. These investors are specifically focused on investing in early-stage companies and are more likely to be willing to take on the higher risk associated with investing in these companies. Classifying a company as early stage will depend on factors like revenue, market presence, customer base, and operational maturity.

More established companies can approach family officers, private equity firms, hedge funds, pension funds, insurance companies and sovereign wealth funds. These investors are typically looking to invest in larger, more established companies with a proven track record.

Companies looking for funding from family offices or strategics should identify family offices and strategics interested in investing in the same industry or sector as their company.

8.4 Is the Investor Right For You

Due diligence on investors is crucial for private company CEOs raising capital. It helps safeguard the company's interests and ensure that the investors chosen fit its vision and goals. CEOs can mitigate risks, build trust, and foster productive partnerships with investors by conducting due diligence.

Investor compatibility

One key aspect of due diligence is to assess investor compatibility. This involves evaluating the investor's investment philosophy, risk appetite, and industry expertise. Identifying investors who share your company's values and vision and who can provide the strategic guidance and support you need to achieve your goals is crucial. Ensure the investment size matches the minimum or maximum investment size for the investor to participate.

Compatibility with investor's portfolio

Suppose the investment proposition is in the same industry or asset class as a significant portion of an investor's existing portfolio. In that case, the investor may want to avoid over-concentration and diversify their holdings more.

Investor's risk appetite

The investor may have other investment opportunities that offer better risk-adjusted returns or align more closely with their objectives. They might prioritise those opportunities.

Right timing

The investor may have personal beliefs, values, or biases that lead them to decline an otherwise suitable investment. Timing can be a crucial factor. The investor might believe the timing is not right for the investment, whether due to market conditions, economic factors, or their current financial position. The investor may lack the resources, such as personnel or expertise, needed to manage the investment effectively.

Tax considerations

Tax implications can be a significant factor in investment decisions. If the investment has unfavourable tax consequences for the investor, they may decide against it.

Legal and ethical considerations

CEOs have a legal and ethical responsibility to ensure that investors are qualified and legitimate. This includes verifying the investor's identity and financial status and conducting a background check to identify potential red flags. Assessing the investor's investment history and track record is also important. Ensure they are not on a sanction list; if a Politically Exposed Person is, more checks will be needed.

Previous investments and exits

Researching an investor's past investments can provide valuable insights into their investment style and approach. Consider the types of companies and industries they have invested in and the successes and failures of their previous investments. This information can help you assess the investor's risk appetite and expertise and identify potential conflicts of interest.

Reputation in the industry

Assessing the investor's reputation and standing within the industry is also essential. Seek references and testimonials from other entrepreneurs who have worked with the investor.

Consider their track record of supporting their portfolio companies and ethical and professional conduct.

Investor involvement

CEOs should also understand the level of involvement that an investor desires. Different investors may have different expectations and goals. Some investors may be more hands-off, while others may want to be more actively involved in the operations. Align expectations and ensure their involvement is in the company's best interests.

Assessing financial capabilities

Another factor to consider is the investor's financial capabilities. This includes assessing their liquidity, net worth, and investment history. It is vital to ensure investors have the financial resources to meet their commitments and support your company's growth.

The hardest is to assess if an investor has money. Investors may choose not to disclose that they have no money or limited funds for several reasons:

- *Maintaining Appearances*: Investors, particularly those with a reputation to uphold, may want to maintain the perception that they are well-capitalized and successful. Admitting financial constraints could damage their image and deter potential investment opportunities in the future.
- *Preserving Negotiating Power:* Investors often negotiate from a position of strength. It could weaken their bargaining power during negotiations if they reveal their financial limitations. They may prefer to keep their financial situation confidential to secure more favourable terms.
- *Market Perception:* Perception can be crucial. If investors admit to financial constraints, it may lead to concerns about

their ability to make successful investments or their current portfolio companies.

- *Privacy and Security:* Some investors may value their financial privacy and security. Revealing their financial status could expose them to unwanted attention or security risks.

- *Future Capital raising:* Investors often participate in multiple funding rounds. Admitting to limited funds could make it challenging for them to raise capital from other sources or attract co-investors for future opportunities.

- *Limited Information Sharing:* Investors may not disclose their financial situation because they prefer to share only the information necessary for a specific transaction. During initial discussions, they may not consider discussing their broader financial position as relevant or appropriate.

Not all investors will keep their financial limitations a secret. In some cases, they may openly communicate their constraints. However, in competitive investment scenarios or when dealing with investors focused on maintaining a strong public image, you may encounter reticence regarding their financial capabilities.

Speak to other entrepreneurs who have worked with the investor to get their insights and feedback. Read industry publications and articles about the investor. This can help you to assess their reputation and track record.

CEOs should continue to monitor their investors after they have invested in the company. This will help identify potential problems or conflicts of interest early on.

What returns is the investor expecting

Investors look for various returns when investing in a private company. The specific return expectations will vary depending on the investor's risk tolerance, investment horizon, and other factors. However, some common return expectations include:

- *High potential for capital appreciation:* Investors in private companies often hope to achieve high returns through capital appreciation, which is an increase in the value of their investment over time. This can happen if the company grows rapidly and becomes more valuable or another company acquires it at a premium.
- *Regular distributions of income:* Some private companies are structured in a way that allows them to distribute income to their investors regularly. This can be an attractive return for investors seeking a steady cash flow stream.
- *Tax benefits:* Investors in private companies may be eligible for certain tax benefits, such as deducting losses from their investments. These tax benefits can make private equity investments more attractive than other investments.
- *Diversification:* Private equity investments can be a valuable way to diversify an investment portfolio. This is because private equity investments are typically not correlated with public markets, which means they can reduce overall portfolio risk.

Investors use a variety of jargon terms when assessing returns. Here are some of the most common terms:

- *IRR (Internal Rate of Return):* The IRR is the rate of return that makes the net present value of all cash flows from an investment equal zero. In other words, the discount rate makes all the cash flows from an investment equivalent to their initial investment.
- *NPV (Net Present Value):* The NPV is the sum of the discounted cash flows from an investment over its lifetime. The discount rate used to discount the cash flows is typically the IRR. A positive NPV indicates that the investment is

expected to generate a return greater than the required rate of return.

- *Multiple:* A multiple is a ratio of a company's valuation to a financial metric, such as revenue, earnings, or cash flow. Multiples are used to compare companies and assess whether a company is overvalued or undervalued.
- *Return on equity (ROE)*: ROE measures a company's profitability and calculates how much profit a company generates with each dollar of shareholder equity. It is calculated by dividing net income by shareholders' equity.
- *Return on assets (ROA):* ROA measures a company's efficiency and calculates how much profit a company generates with each dollar of assets. It is calculated by dividing net income by total assets.
- *Gross margin:* Gross margin is a measure of a company's profitability that calculates the percentage of revenue after deducting the cost of goods sold. It is calculated by dividing gross profit by revenue.
- *Operating margin:* Operating margin is a measure of a company's profitability that calculates the percentage of revenue after deducting all operating expenses. It is calculated by dividing operating income by revenue.
- *EBITDA (Earnings Before Interest, Taxes, Depreciation, and Amortization):* EBITDA measures a company's profitability that excludes certain expenses, such as interest, taxes, depreciation, and amortisation. It often compares companies with different capital structures and tax rates.

There is no guarantee that any investment will generate a return. There is always a risk that investors will lose their entire investment. However, investors in private companies often believe that the potential for high returns outweighs the risks.

Here are some additional factors that investors consider when evaluating the potential returns of a private company investment:

- T*he company's business model*: Investors will carefully evaluate its business model to assess its potential for success. They will consider the size of the market, the company's competitive advantage, and the company's management team.
- *The company's financial performance:* Investors will also review its financial statements to assess its financial performance and health. They will look for revenue growth, profitability, and cash flow.
- *The company's exit strategy:* Investors will also consider its exit strategy, which is how the company plans to provide investors with a return on their investment. This could involve an initial public offering (IPO), an acquisition by another company, or a distribution of cash flow to investors.

Exit strategy alignment

Finally, CEOs should ensure that the investor's exit strategy aligns with the company's long-term goals. Some investors may have a short-term investment horizon, while others may be willing to invest longer. Understand the investor's exit expectations and ensure they align with yours. If the investment lacks a clear exit strategy or the investor is uncertain about how to realise returns, they may hesitate to proceed.

Conducting due diligence on potential investors is a critical aspect of the capital raising process for private company CEOs. By taking the time to assess investor compatibility, legal and ethical considerations, financial capabilities, previous investments and exits, reputation in the industry, investor involvement, and exit strategy alignment, CEOs can make informed, strategic decisions when selecting investors for their ventures.

Different types of investors and their typical exit horizons

- *Angel Investors:* Medium to Long-term. They generally expect an exit within 5 to 7 years, often through a subsequent funding round, acquisition, or IPO.
- *Crowdfunding Investors:* Exit Horizon varies. Exit expectations can be less defined and may depend on the nature of the crowdfunding campaign (equity, reward-based, etc.).
- *Venture Capitalists (VCs)*: Exit Horizon: Medium-term. Their exit horizon usually ranges from 3 to 7 years, with preferred exit strategies including acquisitions or IPOs.
- *Private Equity Firms:* Medium to Long-term. They typically plan for an exit within 4 to 7 years, often through strategic sales or IPOs.
- *Family Offices:* Long-term. They often do not have strict timelines for exits and may stay invested for longer periods, especially if the investment aligns with the family's values and interests.
- *Strategic Investors/Corporate Investors*: Exit Horizon varies widely based on the strategic objectives behind the investment.
- *Hedge Funds*: Short to Medium-term. Hedge funds are often more aggressive and may seek quicker returns through a variety of investment strategies. Their exit horizons can be relatively short, focusing on realising gains within a few years.
- *Pension Funds:* Long-term. They usually have a longer investment horizon and may not prioritise quick exits.

- *Insurance Companies:* Long-term. Similar to pension funds, they manage large pools of capital and typically invest in a way that matches their long-term liability structure. Their exit strategies are often aligned with long-term investment horizons.
- *Sovereign Wealth Funds:* Long-term. They may not have immediate exit expectations and can remain invested for decades, focusing on stable, long-term returns.

Chapter 9 Pitching to Investors

9.1 Approaching Investors

Once you have created a list of potential investors, you must prepare a pitch deck. A pitch deck is a presentation that CEOs use to introduce their business to potential investors. It should be clear, concise, and persuasive. The pitch deck should highlight the company's unique value proposition, target market, financial projections, and management team.

Once you have a pitch deck, you must start pitching to investors. You can pitch to investors in person, over the phone, or via email. It is essential to be prepared to answer any questions investors may have.

Here are some tips for pitching to investors

- Tailor the pitch to your audience. When tailoring your pitch, it is crucial to research your audience thoroughly. Take the time to understand their investment philosophy, previous investments, and any specific sectors or industries they have shown interest in. This information will help you craft a pitch that aligns with their preferences and stands out from the competition.
- Be clear and concise. Investors are busy people, so get to the point quickly.
- Be passionate about your business. Investors want to invest in entrepreneurs who are passionate about their business and believe in its mission.

- Be realistic. Do not overpromise and underdeliver.
- Be prepared to answer questions. Investors will ask you many questions about your business, so be ready to answer them intelligently.
- Be patient. Raising capital takes time. Do not get discouraged if you do not get funded right away.

Raising capital is an essential step for many businesses. CEOs can increase their chances of success by understanding the different types of investors and the factors they consider when making investment decisions.

Who to contact within the organisation

Whether to contact an analyst or a CIO when raising capital depends on several factors.

Chief Investment Officers (CIOs) are responsible for overseeing the investment process for their firms. They typically have a broad understanding of the investment landscape and can provide valuable insights into the types of investments their firms seek. A CIO may be a good contact if you are looking for a general introduction. He will then point you to the right person within his team.

Analysts are responsible for evaluating investment opportunities and making recommendations to their superiors. They typically have a deep understanding of businesses' financial and operational aspects. An analyst may be a good contact if you seek feedback on your business model or financial projections.

If your company is in a specific industry, you should contact analysts and CIOs with expertise. Some analysts and CIOs focus on certain types of investments, such as technology or healthcare. If your company fits into one of these categories, you should try to contact analysts and CIOs with this focus.

Ultimately, the best way to decide who to contact is to do your research, check the backgrounds of the individuals and pitch to the person you believe will best understand the opportunity. This will give you the best chance of finding the right investors for your company.

It is generally not a good idea to reach out to several people on an investor team at once. It can be seen as disrespectful and overwhelming to the investor team. Investors typically have a process for managing incoming inquiries and may prefer to have one point of contact for each company. Reaching out to several people can make it seem like you are not respecting their time or process. It can create confusion and conflict. If you reach out to several people, there is a chance that they will give you conflicting information or advice. If you are unsure who to contact at an investor firm, it is best to err on the side of caution and only contact one person. You can always ask that person to refer you to the appropriate person if necessary.

Reaching out to investors by phone or email

Some investors prefer to be contacted by phone, and others by email. It is essential to respect their preferences and contact them how they like. You can find an investor's preferred contact method on their website or LinkedIn profile. You may also post a hard copy of your pitch to stand out. You can also reach out on other social media platforms if they are not on LinkedIn or find no contact details online.

Choose communication channels that are most effective in reaching each investor segment. For instance, angel investors may be more active on social media platforms, while venture capitalists may prefer traditional methods like email and in-person meetings.

If you are contacting an investor for the first time, it is usually best to email them. This gives them a chance to review your information at their own pace and decide whether or not they are interested in learning more.

You can contact them by phone if you have already established a relationship with an investor. However, it is still a good idea to send them a follow-up email to confirm the details of your conversation.

If you are unsure whether an investor prefers to be contacted by phone or email, you can always email them a brief email asking them how they would like to be contacted.

Does print marketing still have a place

Print marketing can still be an effective tool for capital raising in certain situations. While digital marketing has become increasingly important, print marketing can still offer several benefits. Print materials can convey a sense of credibility and professionalism that can be difficult to replicate in digital marketing. Print materials can last months or years and be easily shared with others. Print marketing can be particularly effective in reaching older investors who may not be as active online.

Here are some specific examples of how print marketing can be used for capital raising:

- Brochures and pitch decks: These materials can give potential investors an overview of your company and its investment potential.
- Newsletters and reports: These materials can be used to keep potential investors informed about your company's progress and achievements.

- Direct mail campaigns: These campaigns can reach a targeted audience of potential investors with a personalised message.
- Print advertising: This can generate interest in your company and its investment potential.

Of course, print marketing is not a magic bullet, and it is important to use it in conjunction with other marketing channels, such as digital marketing and public relations. However, when used effectively, print marketing can be a valuable tool for capital raising.

Make sure your materials are high quality and professional. This will help to convey a sense of credibility and professionalism to potential investors.

Target your materials to a specific audience, your shortlist. Once an investor is interested, sending a hard copy makes you stand out.

How to reach out to investors

- *Personalise your outreach:* Don't send generic emails to investors. Take the time to personalise each email and address the investor by name.
- *Be clear and concise:* State your purpose for reaching out in the first sentence of your email. Investors are busy and don't have time to read long, rambling emails.
- *Highlight your key points:* In the body of your email, highlight the key points about your company, such as your problem, solution, market opportunity, and team.
- *Include a call to action:* Tell the investor what you want them to do next. This could be scheduling a call, visiting your website, or reading your pitch deck.
- *Follow up:* If you don't hear back from an investor after a

week or two, send a follow-up email. Be polite and respectful, but don't be afraid to be persistent.

How to address the investor

The best way to address investors is by their title and last name unless they have explicitly indicated that they prefer to be addressed by their first name. This is the most respectful and professional way to address someone, especially in business. It also helps to avoid any potential confusion or awkwardness.

If you are unsure what title to use, you can always err on the side of caution and use "Mr." or "Ms." followed by their last name. This will help you make a good impression and maintain a professional relationship. You can also research the investor's background to see if they have any specific titles or designations that you should use.

If you have established a more personal relationship with an investor, you may ask them how they prefer to be addressed. However, starting with the more formal title and last name approach is always best until you know their preference.

Use a more formal approach when addressing investors, particularly with family offices, C-level executives, and those in more traditional settings. This demonstrates respect and professionalism, which are crucial for building strong relationships with potential investors.

Use first names when you have established a personal relationship with the investor or if they have explicitly indicated they prefer to be addressed by their first name. You can also use first names when addressing younger investors, particularly in the tech or startup community with a more informal culture.

There are also cultural differences to consider. In Japan, investors tend to use more formal titles and honorifics when addressing each other, while investors in the United States are more comfortable using first names. In Japan, there is a strong emphasis on social hierarchy and respect for elders and superiors. This is reflected in formal titles and honorifics, which indicate one's place in the social order. On the other hand, the United States has a more informal and egalitarian culture. This is reflected in the use of first names, seen as a way of showing equality and friendliness. Americans are generally more comfortable using first names, even when addressing people they do not know well.

The importance of drip-feeding documentation

Drip-feeding information is a strategic approach for engaging investors and ensuring your message resonates effectively. It involves gradually releasing information over time rather than overwhelming them with a large amount of data at once. This method has several benefits:

- *Enhanced Comprehension and Retention:* Investors are more likely to remember and process information when presented in smaller, more manageable chunks. By drip-feeding information, you allow them to absorb each piece gradually, reducing the risk of information overload and ensuring better comprehension.
- *Maintained Interest and Engagement:* Drip-feeding information keeps investors eager for more. Each release of new information sparks their curiosity, prompting them to stay tuned for the next instalment. This continuous engagement ensures that your message stays top-of-mind.
- *Building Anticipation and Excitement:* By strategically withholding some information, you create a sense of anticipation and excitement among investors. They eagerly

await each new release, making the information more impactful when finally revealed.

- *Tailored to Investor Preferences:* Investors have different preferences for consuming information. Some prefer to receive it in small doses, while others may want to delve into larger amounts at once. Drip-feeding allows you to cater to these diverse preferences, ensuring that investors receive information the way they prefer.

- *Adapting to Investor Feedback:* Drip-feeding allows you to gauge investor reactions and adapt your messaging accordingly. As you release information, you can observe how investors respond, adjusting your approach based on their feedback.

- *Managing the Pace of Information Release:* Managing the pace of information release is crucial in a rapidly evolving business landscape. Drip-feeding lets you control the narrative, ensuring you reveal information at the right time and most effectively.

- *Maintaining Control over the Message:* Drip-feeding prevents misinterpretation of information. Controlling the flow of information ensures that your message is delivered consistently and accurately.

- *Creating a Sense of Exclusivity:* By selectively releasing information, you create a sense of exclusivity among investors. They feel privileged to receive insider insights, fostering a stronger connection with your company.

- *Nurturing Relationships with Investors:* Drip-feeding information provides opportunities to interact with investors regularly, building stronger relationships over time. This ongoing communication fosters trust and loyalty among investors.

- *Sustained Interest beyond Initial Campaign:* Drip-feeding information extends the lifespan of your investor outreach efforts. You maintain investor interest and engagement by providing valuable insights after the initial campaign.

What can affect how many investors you need to contact

If you have a strong network of investors, you may be able to close your round with fewer investors. However, if you are new to capital raising, you may need to contact more investors to find the right ones for your company.

If you are in a highly competitive industry, you may need to reach out to more investors to find the right ones. If the industry is out of favour and investors do not consider the timing right, finding an investor may take much longer.

Early-stage companies may need to reach out to more investors than later-stage companies. Investors are generally more risk-averse when investing in early-stage companies, so they may be more selective.

If you are raising a large round, you will need to reach out to more investors than if you are raising a small round. It is more difficult to find multiple investors willing to invest a large amount of money in the same company.

Rejection is part of the process

According to different studies, 90% of startups fail. Investors turn down 90% of startup pitches. This is a high rejection rate. There are several reasons why investors might turn down a pitch. Some of the most common reasons include:

- The business idea is not feasible or scalable.
- The team is not experienced enough or does not have the right skills.
- The market is too small or too competitive.

- The valuation is too high.
- The pitch is not well-delivered or does not address the investor's concerns.
- The pitch does not fit their investment criteria.

Getting more rejections when capital raising is better than not hearing back. Each rejection is an opportunity to learn and improve your pitch. If an investor takes the time to respond to you, it means that they were interested in your pitch, but it just wasn't a good fit for them. This is good because it means you are on the right track and pitching to the right investors.

Don't take it personally. Rejection is a normal part of the capital raising process. Learn from each rejection. Try to figure out what you could have done differently. Keep moving forward. Don't let rejection discourage you, and be persistent. The more you pitch, the more likely you are to get funded.

What to do when an investor does not respond to emails

There are several reasons investors may have yet to respond to emails.

Investors are busy people. They receive hundreds of emails from entrepreneurs daily and do not have time to respond to every incoming email.

Investors have specific investment theses and interests. They are unlikely to respond if your company does not fall within their investment and your email is poorly written or unprofessional.

Investors are more likely to respond to emails that are well-written and professional. If your email is poorly written or amateurish, they will likely ignore it. Proofread your email carefully. Make sure there are no errors in grammar or spelling.

Some investors have specific instructions for entrepreneurs who are interested in pitching them. They may ask you to fill out a standard application on their website. They are more likely to ignore your email if you do not follow their instructions.

Investors are more likely to respond to personalised e-mails specific to them. If your email is too generic, they will likely ignore it.

Be prepared to follow up. If you are still waiting to hear back from an investor after a week or two, sending a follow-up email is okay. However, don't be too persistent. If you send multiple follow-up emails, you will annoy the investor, and they are even less likely to respond.

Calling investors

It is often a good idea to pick up the phone and follow up with an investor if you haven't heard back from them in a while and you genuinely believe there is a good fit. Many investors are busy and may not always have the time to respond to emails right away. A phone call can help to get their attention and remind them of your pitch. When you call an investor, be polite and professional. Briefly introduce yourself and remind them of your email. Ask if they have any questions about your pitch. If they are interested in moving forward, ask if they would be willing to schedule a meeting. In many cases, the investor will apologise for not immediately responding.

Choose a time during the investor's work hours. This is usually between 9 am and 5 pm on weekdays. Avoid calling too early or too late: Early morning calls can be disruptive, and late evening calls may catch the investor after they have already left for the day. Consider the investor's time zone: If the investor is in a different time zone, adjust your call time accordingly. Send the investor a brief email in advance: Let the investor know that you will be calling them and ask for a time that would be convenient for them. Respect the investor's time and keep your call concise and to the point.

Specific times that may be good to call investors

- 9 am to 10 am: This is often an excellent time to catch investors before they have gotten too busy with their day.
- 11 am to 12 pm: This is another good time to catch investors, as they may be finishing up their morning tasks.
- 2 pm to 3 pm: This is a good time to call investors after they have had lunch and are back at their desks.
- 4 pm to 5 pm: This may be a good time to catch investors before they leave for the day.
- When pitching in the Middle East, keep in mind prayer times.

What turns investors off

Investors see many pitches and have developed a keen eye for red flags.

Investors want to see that you have a realistic understanding of the market, your competition, and your company's capabilities. Investors will quickly tune out if you make unrealistic claims about your potential growth or profits.

It is obvious when a founder hasn't done their homework. Investors will question whether you're ready to lead a company if you can't answer basic questions about your business or market.

Investors want to know why your company differs from the competition and why they should invest in you. If you can't clearly articulate your value proposition, investors will hesitate to give you their money.

Investors need to see that you have a solid understanding of your financial needs and how you plan to use their money. If you're vague about your financials, investors will be concerned about your ability to manage the company's finances.

Your pitch is your chance to make a good first impression on investors. Investors will not be impressed if your presentation is poorly organised, unprofessional, or boring.

Investors want to see that you are passionate about your business. How can you expect investors to be if you're not excited about your own company? Investors are very sensitive to dishonesty and will quickly spot any red flags. You will lose investors' trust and damage your reputation if caught lying or exaggerating. Investors expect founders to be professional, courteous, and respectful. You'll make a bad impression on investors if you're rude, dismissive, or arrogant.

Investors want to see that you have a realistic understanding of your company's valuation. Investors will hesitate to invest if you ask for an unrealistic amount.

Investors will often ask tough questions, and you need to handle them with grace and composure. Investors will question your ability to lead the company if you get flustered or defensive.

9.2 Targeting Different Geographical Markets

Raising capital can be challenging for any CEO, but it can be tough if you are trying to raise capital in a different geographic market. In addition to the cultural differences, there are several factors to consider, such as the regulatory environment and the investment landscape.

The first step in raising capital in a different geographic market is understanding the regulatory environment. This includes understanding the laws and regulations governing securities offerings and investments. Understand the tax implications of raising capital in a different geographic market. It is essential to consult with an attorney and a tax advisor to ensure that you comply with all applicable laws and regulations. Learn about the regulatory environment, the culture, and the investment landscape in the geographic market where you are trying to raise capital.

Cultural differences can impact how investors communicate, make decisions, and value businesses. Understanding these differences is essential for successful cross-border capital raising. Conduct thorough research on the target market's cultural norms and business practices before initiating capital raising efforts. Consider working with a local partner who can provide insights into local customs and help build relationships with potential investors. Assemble a team of experienced advisors, including lawyers, accountants, and investment bankers, who are familiar with the cultural nuances and can assist with compliance. Adapt your communication style to align with the preferences of investors in the target market. Recognise that different cultures may prefer various levels of formality and directness.

Be aware of risk tolerance differences and how investors in the target market approach valuation and investment time horizons. Tailor your investment documentation to meet the preferences of investors in the target market. This includes considering the level of detail, language, and presentation style. Be aware of potential differences in terminology and the interpretation of terms in different countries. What may be considered non-binding in one country could have different implications elsewhere.

9.3 Cross-Border Cultural Sensitivity

Be aware of the cultural differences between countries and regions when capital raising cross-border. By understanding and navigating cultural differences, private companies can increase their chances of success in raising capital from international investors.

There are several reasons why cultural sensitivity is important in cross-border capital raising. Cultural differences can impact how investors communicate and make decisions. For example, investors in some cultures may prefer to speak more formally than investors in others. Investors in some cultures may also be more risk-averse than investors in others. Cultural differences can impact the way that businesses are valued. For example, investors in some cultures may place a higher value on intangible assets, such as brand recognition and intellectual property, than investors in other cultures.

Navigating cultural differences

There are several things that private companies can do to navigate cultural differences in cross-border capital raising.

Before you start capital raising cross-border, research the cultural norms and business practices in the countries where you seek to raise capital. This will help you understand how to communicate with potential investors and structure your capital raising efforts in a culturally appropriate way.

Working with a local partner can be helpful when capital raising is cross-border. A local partner can help you understand the cultural norms and business practices in the country where you raise capital. A local partner can also help you to identify potential investors and build relationships with them.

Work with a team of experienced advisors, such as lawyers, accountants, and investment bankers, when capital raising cross-border. Your advisors can help you navigate the cultural differences and comply with all applicable regulations.

Be patient and respectful. It is important to be patient and respectful when capital raising is cross-border. Building relationships with potential investors in other countries may take longer. Be respectful of cultural differences and avoid making assumptions about potential investors based on their cultural background.

Cultural differences in communication styles

American investors often prefer direct and assertive communication. They appreciate concise and well-structured pitches that highlight the potential return on investment. They value data-driven analyses and expect entrepreneurs to present a compelling business case.

British investors appreciate a more formal and reserved communication style. They value professionalism, thoroughness, and attention to detail. It is essential to provide comprehensive documentation supporting your business plans and projections.

German investors typically favour a highly structured and detail-oriented approach. They appreciate thorough research, extensive due diligence, and a focus on risk mitigation strategies. It is crucial to provide comprehensive financial projections and demonstrate a solid understanding of the market.

Chinese investors often place emphasis on building strong personal relationships before making investment decisions. Networking and establishing trust are crucial in this market. Chinese investors may prefer face-to-face meetings to get to know the entrepreneur personally.

Japanese investors value respect, politeness, and harmony in business interactions. They may prefer to communicate more indirectly and formally than investors in other cultures, such as the United States. They tend to have a long-term perspective and may focus more on the reputation and character of the entrepreneur rather than short-term gains. Building trust through multiple meetings is important in this culture.

Investors in the Middle East appreciate personalised relationships based on trust and mutual respect. Business discussions may be more relaxed and involve getting to know each other personally before delving into specific investment opportunity details. Middle Eastern investors value hospitality and socialising.

Australian investors appreciate a straightforward and down-to-earth communication style. They value honesty, transparency, and directness in pitches and discussions. It is important to present clear financial projections and demonstrate a solid understanding of the local market dynamics.

Brazilian investors tend to have a more informal communication style characterised by warmth, enthusiasm, and passion. Building personal relationships is key in this market, as Brazilians value trust before making investment decisions. Presenting your pitch with energy and showcasing your commitment can help establish credibility.

Cultural differences in Investment style

Investors in some cultures, such as Germany, may be more risk-averse than investors in other cultures, such as the United States. Investors in South Korea are also more risk-averse than investors in other developed countries, such as the United States and the United Kingdom. This is likely due to the country's Confucian culture, which emphasises stability and predictability.

Investors in the United States may exhibit higher risk tolerance and be more open to investing in volatile markets. Investors in India tend to be more risk-tolerant than investors in other developing countries, such as Brazil and Russia. This is likely due to the country's young population and growing economy.

Investors in some cultures, such as China, may place a higher value on intangible assets, such as brand recognition and intellectual property, than investors in other cultures, such as the United States. In the United States, valuation is the process of determining the worth of a company. This may involve various methods, such as discounted cash flow or comparable company analysis. However, valuation may be more subjective in countries like Japan. Investors in these countries may be more likely to rely on their judgment and experience when determining the value of a company. Investors in France tend to place a higher value on the quality of earnings and cash flow than investors in other developed countries. This is likely due to the country's civil law system, which protects shareholders more. Investors in Australia tend to place a higher value on natural resources and commodities than investors in other developed countries. This is likely due to the country's rich endowment of natural resources.

Cultural differences can also impact investment time horizons. In some cultures, there may be a focus on long-term investments with a patient approach towards generating returns over an extended period. On the other hand, some cultures might prioritise short-term gains and have a more opportunistic outlook. Investors in Canada tend to have a long-term investment horizon, similar to investors in Japan. This is likely due to the country's relatively stable economy and culture of valuing financial security.

An exit strategy is a plan for how an investor will sell their stake in a company. In the United States, investors typically expect to exit an investment within five to seven years. However, in other countries, such as China, investors may be willing to hold onto their investments for longer periods.

Be prepared to negotiate. It is important to be prepared to negotiate with potential investors. Investors in other countries may have different expectations about the terms of the investment than investors in your home country. Some cultures may emphasise building personal relationships before entering business agreements, while others prefer a more direct and concise approach.

These are generalisations, and individual preferences can vary within each country's investor community. When raising capital internationally, adapting your communication style to align with the cultural expectations of the target market can significantly improve your chances of success.

Cultural differences in views on presentation materials

Investors from different countries may have different preferences regarding investment documentation. For example, some investors prefer more detailed documentation, while others prefer a more concise summary. Some investors may prefer documentation in English, while others may prefer documentation in their native language.

Japanese investors tend to prefer detailed investment documentation that is presented in a formal and respectful manner. They may also prefer documentation that is translated into Japanese.

Chinese investors value relationships and personal trust highly. As a result, they may prefer investment documentation that is presented in a way that builds rapport and emphasises the team behind the investment opportunity.

German investors tend to be risk-averse and prefer to invest in well-established companies with a proven track record. As a result, they prefer investment documentation that is very detailed and provides a comprehensive overview of the company's financials and business model.

US investors are more risk-tolerant and are willing to invest in early-stage companies with high growth potential. As a result, they may prefer investment documentation that is more concise and focuses on the company's vision and market opportunity.

Different meanings in terminology

A non-binding term sheet in one country may be called something else in another. In the United States, a term sheet is a non-binding agreement that outlines the key terms of an investment. It is typically used as a starting point for negotiating the final investment agreement. However, a term sheet may be considered more binding in some other countries, such as China and Japan. In these countries, investors may expect the term sheet to be finalised before moving on to the next stage of the investment process.

9.4 Operating in Different Economic Conditions

Raising capital can be challenging in any economic climate, but it can be challenging during a downturn. Investors are typically more risk-averse during a recession and may be less likely to invest in startups or early-stage companies. However, there are still ways to raise capital during a recession.

In a bull market

- *Take advantage of investor confidence.* Investors are typically more confident and willing to take risks in a bull market. This can be an excellent time to raise capital, especially if you are a startup or early-stage company.
- *Focus on growth.* Investors are looking for companies that are snowballing in a bull market. Remember to highlight your company's growth potential in your pitch deck and marketing materials.
- *Do not be afraid to ask for a high valuation:* Investors typically pay a higher valuation for companies with solid growth potential.

In a bear market

- *Focus on your fundamentals.* Investors focus more on fundamentals during a bear market, such as revenue, profitability, and cash flow. Remember to highlight your company's strong fundamentals in your pitch deck and marketing materials.
- *Be conservative with your valuation.* Investors are typically more risk-averse during a bear market, so it's important to be conservative with your valuation. You may need to accept a lower valuation than you would in a bull market.
- *Be prepared to negotiate.* Investors may be more likely to negotiate on the terms of the investment during a recession. Be ready to negotiate on the valuation, ownership structure, and other key terms.
- *Be patient.* It may take longer to raise capital during a bear market. Be prepared to spend more time networking with investors and building relationships.

- *Look for alternative sources of funding.* Many alternative funding sources, such as crowdfunding platforms, angel investors, and venture debt, are available. Consider these funding sources if you struggle to raise capital from traditional investors.

In a recession

- *Focus on your strengths.* What makes your company unique and attractive to investors? Highlight your strengths in your pitch deck and marketing materials.
- *Focus on your runway.* Investors are more concerned about a company's runway during a recession. Remember to highlight your company's runway in your pitch deck and marketing materials. A runway of more than a year is advisable.
- *Be realistic about your valuation.* Investors are more likely to invest in companies that are realistically valued. Do not overvalue your company, or you may scare away potential investors.
- *Be transparent about your challenges.* Investors understand that companies face challenges during a recession. Be transparent about your challenges and how you plan to overcome them.
- *Consider alternative sources of funding.* It may be challenging to raise capital from traditional investors during a recession. Consider alternative funding sources, such as crowdfunding platforms, angel investors, and venture debt.

9.5 A Numbers Game – Key Metrics

Capital raising can be seen as a numbers game. Founders and entrepreneurs must meet with many different investors before securing funding. Data analysis gives important feedback to improve.

When capital raising, track how many investors read your email. This will give you an idea of how effective your email outreach is. You can follow the open rate of your emails using an email marketing platform such as Mailchimp or Constant Contact. The average email open rate for capital raising emails is around 20-30%. If you send out 100 emails, you can expect about 20-30 investors to open them.

Another critical metric to track is the response rate to your email. This will give you an idea of how interested investors are in your company. The average response rate for capital raising emails is around 5-10%. If you send out 100 emails, you can expect about 5-10 investors to respond. Having relationships will improve the response ratio.

The final metric to track is the percentage of investors meeting with you. This is the most important metric, the most direct indicator of investor interest. The average percentage of investors meeting with founders is around 1-2%. This means that if you send out 100 emails, you can expect 1-2 investors to take a meeting with you.

You cannot bank on every meeting converting. There may only be one in ten meetings, in which case, you must reach out to 1000 investors to convert one.

Improving your key metrics

- *Personalise your emails.* Investors are more likely to respond to personalised emails than generic emails. When sending out capital raising emails, personalise the email to each investor. You can mention something specific about their interests or investment thesis.

- *Segment your email list.* Not all investors are the same. Some investors are more interested in early-stage companies, while others are more interested in later-stage companies. Some investors focus more on specific industries, while others are more generalist. It is crucial to segment your email list so that you can send targeted emails to different groups of investors.

- *Write clear and concise emails.* Investors are busy people. They don't have time to read long, rambling emails. When writing capital raising emails, be sure to be clear and concise. Get to the point quickly and make it easy for investors to understand your request. Do not dump all your documentation on the investor in one go. Drip feed them information.

- *Follow up with investors.* If you don't hear back from an investor after a week or two, follow up with them. A gentle follow-up email can be all it takes to get an investor's attention.

How capital raising experts interpret these numbers

Capital raising experts use these numbers to track their progress and adjust their capital raising strategy as needed. For example, if an expert notices that their email open rate is low, they may need to try different subject lines or email content. If an expert sees that their response rate is low, they may need to improve their email personalisation or segmentation. And if an expert notices that their meeting percentage is low, they may need to improve their pitch deck or networking.

By tracking these numbers, capital raising experts can improve their chances of success and raise the capital they need to grow their businesses. They also will quickly understand how difficult capital raising is by the response ratio. Higher response ratios will indicate a shorter selling cycle.

Additional tips for improving your capital raising numbers:

- Use a CRM system. A CRM system can help you track your email outreach and investor interactions. This will give you insights into what is working and what is not.
- Get feedback from investors. After each meeting with an investor, ask them for feedback. This feedback can help you improve your pitch deck and your networking skills.
- Don't give up. It takes time and effort to raise capital. Don't get discouraged if you don't hear back from investors right away. Keep following up and keep networking.

Tracking and improving your capital raising numbers can increase your chances of success and raise the capital you need to grow your business. However, capital raising is not simply a numbers game. Building relationships with investors and convincing them that your company is a good investment is also essential. This can be done by developing a strong pitch deck, networking with investors, and participating in pitch competitions.

Here are some tips for capital raising that go beyond simply playing a numbers game:

- *Target the right investors.* Not all investors are the same. Some investors are more interested in early-stage companies, while others are more interested in later-stage companies. Some investors focus more on specific industries, while others are generalists. Targeting investors who are likely to be interested in your company and your investment opportunity is important.

- *Build relationships with investors.* Investors are more likely to invest in companies they have a relationship with. Try to get to know potential investors and build relationships with them. This can be done by attending industry events, networking online, and contacting investors directly.
- *Tell a compelling story.* Investors want to invest in companies with a compelling story. Ensure your pitch deck is well-written and tells a story about your company, product or service, and team.
- *Be prepared to answer questions.* Investors will have questions about your company and your investment opportunity. Be prepared to answer these questions honestly and intelligently.

Chapter 10 Mastering Presentation Dynamics

10.1 Rehearsing Tone and Body Language

Your pitch to investors is one of your most important presentations. It is your chance to make a great first impression and convince investors to put their money in your company. To deliver a successful pitch, you need to be well-prepared and confident. You also must connect with your audience and deliver your message clearly and concisely. It is about the tone, the body language and the connection.

Common presentation styles that do not work

- **Death by PowerPoint:** The presenter spends the entire meeting reading off slides. This is incredibly boring and ineffective. Investors want to hear you talk about your business rather than read about it.
- **Winging It:** The presenter does not have a prepared presentation and wings it. This is also unprofessional and makes you look like you don't know what you're talking about.
- **The Rambler:** The presenter talks without getting to the point. This frustrates investors and makes it difficult for them to understand your business.
- **Nervous Nelly:** The presenter is so nervous they cannot speak clearly or think straight. This is not a good impression to make on investors.

- **Arrogant Know-It-All:** The presenter comes across as arrogant and thinks they know everything. Investors do not want to invest in someone not open to feedback or new ideas.

Verbal delivery

The best way to prepare for your pitch is to rehearse it repeatedly. This will help you to memorise your material and deliver it smoothly.

Speak at a moderate pace. Don't speak too fast or too slow. Speak at a pace that is easy for your audience to understand. Speak clearly and slowly. English may not be everyone's first language. Get to the point quickly and avoid using jargon or technical language. Use simple words. Pitch at the level of a 12-year-old even if the investor has a PhD.

Make sure that your pitch is the right length. Investors are typically busy, so you don't want to waste their time. A good rule of thumb is to aim for a pitch that is 10-15 minutes long, leaving time for questions.

Your tone of voice is essential when delivering your pitch. You want to sound confident and enthusiastic, but you do not want to be arrogant or pushy. Speak with a strong voice, using positive intonation. Vary your pitch and volume to add interest and keep your audience engaged. You can also use pauses and silence to emphasise important points. Cary the tone of your voice and convey passion. Speaking monotonously, avoiding eye contact, or having a negative facial expression may make investors think you are not passionate about the business.

Filler words, such as "um," "like," and "you know" can be distracting and make you seem unprofessional. Try to eliminate filler words from your speech.

Believe in your company and your vision. Investors can tell if you are not passionate about your business. Focus on your company's potential and opportunities. Avoid talking about problems or challenges.

Mirror the investor. When someone verbally acknowledges and repeats the other person's statement, they demonstrate that they value what was shared.

It is crucial to be aware that the more we manifest defensive, apologetic, and self-deprecating tendencies, the more likely we will attract unwarranted criticism and derogatory remarks. This unhealthy cycle can quickly take hold. When others make us feel like losers, it becomes increasingly difficult not to internalise those beliefs. Stop saying sorry!

Body language

Body language is a key aspect of non-verbal communication. While words convey explicit messages, non-verbal cues like body language communicate implicit information about emotions, attitudes, and intentions. This can include gestures, facial expressions, posture, and even proximity to others.

Often, body language either reinforces what is being said or contradicts it. A person might verbally agree, but their crossed arms and averted gaze might suggest discomfort or disagreement. In such cases, body language provides additional context that might be more truthful than spoken words.

Some elements of body language are universal and can be understood across different cultures. For example, smiles and frowns convey similar emotions globally. This universality makes body language a powerful tool in communication, especially in diverse or international contexts.

Body language is often an involuntary reaction to emotional states. It can reveal feelings like nervousness, confidence, openness, or defensiveness. For instance, someone who is nervous might fidget or avoid eye contact. Effective use of body language can help in building rapport and trust. Mirroring someone's body language, maintaining appropriate eye contact, and using open gestures can create a sense of empathy and understanding.

Body language plays a role in the flow of conversations. Non-verbal cues can signal when speaking or listening is appropriate and help manage turn-taking in discussions.

While the exact percentage of non-verbal communication varies, and the "less than 10 per cent" figure for verbal communication might be a bit simplistic, it is clear that body language is a significant component of effective communication.

Understanding and appropriately using body language can significantly enhance the effectiveness of interactions. You want to project confidence and enthusiasm, but you also want to be professional and respectful.

Tips for effective body language

Make eye contact. Eye contact is a powerful tool that can help you connect with your audience and make them feel like you are speaking directly to them. Aim to make eye contact with different members of the audience throughout your presentation. This will help to keep everyone engaged and make you seem more confident and personable. An excessive amount of direct eye contact could be intimidating. An intense stare could cause others to feel uncomfortable, with them maybe even questioning your overall sanity. Staring, in some cultures, might be viewed as rude.

Sit and stand straight. Good posture is another key to projecting confidence. Sit and stand up straight with your shoulders back and your head held high. This will make you look and feel more poised and professional. It will also improve your breathing so you can speak more clearly and confidently.

Smile. Smiling is a simple way to make yourself more approachable and likeable. It also helps to create a positive atmosphere that will put your audience at ease. However, make sure your smile is genuine and not forced. A fake smile can come across as insincere and make you seem untrustworthy.

Avoid fidgeting. Fidgeting is a sign of nervousness and can distract your audience from your presentation. Keep your hands still, and avoid playing with your hair, clicking your pen, or bouncing your foot. If you fidget, take a deep breath and focus on your message.

Use open gestures. Do not cross the arms or legs. Open gestures, such as spreading your arms or using your hands to illustrate your points, can help to make your presentation more engaging. However, avoid using gestures that are too large or exaggerated. These can make you seem overly animated and distract your audience from your message.

Nod your head in agreement. Nodding your head in agreement is a subtle way to show that you listen attentively and agree with what the other person is saying. This can help to build rapport and trust with your audience.

Mirroring. Be aware of the other person's body language and harmonise with it where appropriate, but do not overdo it or deliberately copy it. Techniques such as mirroring body language, matching speech patterns, and using similar terminology can help create a connection with investors, making them more receptive to the pitch.

Lean forward slightly to show interest. Leaning forward slightly when the other person is speaking shows that you are interested in what they have to say. This can also help to make you seem more engaged and enthusiastic.

Some examples of body language cues that investors find off-putting are slouching, avoiding eye contact, fidgeting with your hands, crossed arms, and pacing back and forth.

Displaying submissive body language can inadvertently communicate feelings of inadequacy. This includes quietness, nervousness, slumping posture, defensive gestures, and self-consciousness.

10.2 Storytelling and Emotional Appeal

When raising capital, CEOs and entrepreneurs often focus on the analytical aspects of their pitch. They meticulously prepare their financials, market research, and competitive analysis, which are undoubtedly crucial. However, they sometimes overlook the power of storytelling and emotional appeal. Facts and figures matter in the business, but emotions can drive investors to believe in your vision and open their wallets. This chapter will explore the art of storytelling and emotional appeal in capital raising. We will highlight why it matters, how to do it effectively, and how it can impact your capital raising success.

The power of storytelling

Stories are the oldest form of communication known to humanity. They have been used to convey information, inspire, and connect people for thousands of years. In the context of capital raising, storytelling serves several essential purposes.

Stories capture the audience's attention. They draw listeners in and create a connection that transcends mere data.

Complex business concepts can be simplified and made more accessible through storytelling. A well-crafted story can clarify your value proposition and the problem you're solving.

People remember stories far better than facts and figures. If your story is compelling, investors are more likely to recall and share it with others.

Stories evoke emotions, and emotions drive decision-making. By telling a story that resonates emotionally, you can influence investors' feelings and, ultimately, their actions.

The emotional appeal

Emotions play a pivotal role in decision-making, including investment decisions. Investors are not just looking at the potential return on investment but also considering how they feel about the opportunity.

Your passion for your business is contagious. Communicating your unwavering dedication and belief in your vision can ignite a similar passion in your potential investors.

Building trust is essential. Investors need to trust not only your competence but also your integrity. Emotional appeal helps to convey trustworthiness.

Your enthusiasm for the opportunity can be infectious. Investors are also more likely to get excited when you're excited about your business. Gestures can accentuate a conversation and excite, used in moderation.

By sharing relatable stories, you can generate empathy. When investors can empathise with your target market or the problem you're solving, they become more invested in your success.

Investors seek opportunities that offer hope for a brighter future. Your story should instil hope that your business can achieve something meaningful.

Crafting your capital raising story

- *Know Your Audience:* Understand your investors. What motivates them? What are their values? Tailor your story to resonate with your specific audience.
- *Identify Your Key Messages*: What are the most critical points you want to convey? Your story should revolve around these key messages.
- *Create a Hero's Journey:* Your business, and by extension, you, are the hero of your story. Frame your journey as a hero's journey with challenges, setbacks, and ultimate triumph.
- *Use Relatable Characters:* Introduce characters that your audience can relate to. This might include customers whose lives have been transformed by your product or employees who are deeply committed to your mission.
- *Highlight the Problem:* Begin with the problem you're solving. Make it relatable and evoke empathy. Share real stories or statistics that illustrate the issue.
- *Share Your Vision*: Describe your vision for solving the problem. Paint a vivid picture of what the world will look like once your solution is in place.
- *Reveal Your Passion:* Show your passion for your business. Investors should see that you're not just in it for the money but because you genuinely care about the impact you're making.
- *Showcase Successes:* Highlight milestones and successes you've achieved. Share stories of how you've overcome obstacles and adapted to changing circumstances.
- *Create a Sense of Urgency:* Convey why this is the right investment time. Share opportunities and market trends that make your business poised for success.
- *End with a Call to Action:* Every good story has a conclusion.

In your pitch, this is your call to action. Clearly state what you are asking of the investor and why they should act now.

Explore using visual aids in your pitch, such as photos, videos, or infographics. Visual elements can be powerful tools for conveying emotion and bringing your story to life. Strike the right balance between emotional appeal and data-driven content. While emotions make your pitch memorable, data and facts provide credibility and justification for investment.

Common hurdles and how to overcome them

- *Authenticity:* Your story must be authentic. Exaggerating or fabricating details can damage trust. Focus on genuine experiences and emotions.
- *Clarity:* Storytelling can simplify complex ideas, but striking a balance is crucial. Your story should make your pitch more accessible, not convoluted.
- *Relevance:* Ensure that your story is relevant to your business. It should align with your mission, values, and objectives. A story that feels forced or unrelated can backfire.
- *Timing:* Be mindful of the timing of your emotional appeal. It should complement your key messages, not overwhelm them.
- *Overcoming Scepticism:* Some investors may be naturally sceptical of emotional appeals. Back up your story with data and facts to provide a well-rounded pitch.

Measuring the success of storytelling and emotional appeal

Are investors actively engaged during your pitch? Are they

asking questions and showing interest beyond the numbers? Any questions, including critical ones, are good questions. You must worry if an investor does not ask you a single question.

Listen to the feedback you receive. If investors comment on the emotional resonance of your story, take it as a positive sign.

Ultimately, the success of your pitch can be measured by whether investors choose to invest. If your pitch moves them emotionally and convinces them of your vision, it will likely lead to investment.

Emotional appeal is not just about securing initial investment; it's also about retaining investors. Building emotional connections can lead to long-term support.

Storytelling and emotional appeal are potent tools in the capital raising arsenal. They can set you apart from the competition, create a lasting impression, and inspire investors to join your entrepreneurial journey. While the numbers and data provide a rational basis for investment, emotions often tip the scales in your favour.

So, as you prepare your next capital raising pitch, remember to craft a story that resonates, engages, and moves your audience emotionally. It might be the most persuasive aspect of your presentation, leading to the financial backing you need to turn your vision into reality.

10.3 How to Be Passionate Without Sounding Fake

Being passionate without sounding fake can be challenging, but it's important to remember that investors are looking for genuinely excited people about their ideas.

The more you know about your product, service, or idea, the more naturally your passion will shine through. Be prepared to answer potential investors' questions, and don't be afraid to get technical if the situation calls for it.

Don't just recite a memorised pitch. Discuss your passion for your venture and why you believe in its potential. Let your enthusiasm shine through in your voice and body language.

Stories are a powerful way to connect with people on an emotional level. Share stories about how your product or service has helped others or about the challenges you've overcome in bringing your vision to life.

Do not try to be someone you are not. Investors can spot a fake a mile away, so be true to yourself and your passion. The more you practice your pitch, the more comfortable and confident you will become. This will help you come across as more authentic and passionate.

Avoid clichés and buzzwords. These phrases are overused and can make you sound insincere. Instead, use your own words to express your passion.

Do not over-hype your product or service. Be honest about its strengths and weaknesses. Investors will appreciate your honesty and will be more likely to believe in your vision.

Avoid making promises you cannot keep. Do not overstate your company's potential or make guarantees you cannot fulfil. This will only damage your credibility.

Be humble. Don't come across as arrogant or cocky. Investors are more likely to invest in people who are humble and willing to learn.

Be prepared for questions. Investors will likely question your product, service, or business model. Be prepared to answer these questions clearly and concisely.

10.4 Bonding with Investors

Factors that will help you establish a relationship with investors are charisma, sharing personal information, creating rapport, showing empathy and effortlessly connecting.

- **Charisma:** Charisma is a magnetic quality that makes individuals stand out and attracts others to them. It often involves confidence and is not necessarily an innate trait. Charismatic people significantly influence those around them and are often seen as leaders.
- **Sharing Personal Information:** Willingly sharing information about oneself to others. You encourage others to do the same by opening up and fostering a deeper understanding and connection. It is a give-and-take process that can enhance relational dynamics.
- **Creating Rapport**: Creating a sense of comfort and connection with others. Building bonds through common interests that can be relied upon in future interactions. Rapport is fundamental to successful communication as it establishes trust and understanding.
- **Empathy:** Empathy refers to understanding and sharing another person's feelings to see situations from their perspective. This skill requires attentive listening and observing without judgment and often involves mirroring body language to make others feel more relaxed and understood.
- **Connecting effortlessly:** Synergy occurs when there is an effortless connection between people, where understanding and communication flow naturally. Body language and non-verbal cues often communicate as effectively as words in such relationships.

10.5 Dress Rehearsal

First impressions matter, especially when trying to raise money from investors. Your dress code can greatly influence how investors perceive you and your company. No matter what you choose to wear, make sure you feel comfortable and confident in your outfit. This will help you to project a professional image to investors.

Do

- Dress professionally. This means wearing clean, well-fitting clothes appropriate for a business setting. Avoid anything too casual, such as jeans, shorts, or T-shirts.
- Choose classic colours and styles. Black, navy, and grey are always good choices. Avoid anything too trendy or flashy.
- Choose clothes that fit well. Clothes that are too tight or too loose will make you look unprofessional.
- Pay attention to the details. Ensure your clothes are clean and pressed, your hair is neat, and your shoes are polished.
- Accessorise wisely. A simple scarf or watch can add a touch of personality to your outfit.
- Be yourself. Do not try to be someone you are not. Investors will appreciate your authenticity.
- For men: A suit, blazer, and slacks are classic and professional. You can also wear a dress shirt and tie with khakis or chinos.
- For women: A dress or skirt suit is a good option for women. You can also wear dress pants with a blouse or sweater.

Don't

- Overdress. You do not want to look like you are trying too hard. Aim for a look that is both professional and approachable.

- Underdress. Dressing too casually can make you look unprofessional and unprepared.
- Wear anything too revealing or too tight. You want investors to focus on your business, not your outfit.
- Wear too much jewellery or makeup: Avoid wearing too much jewellery or makeup, as this can be distracting and unprofessional. A simple, understated look is best.
- Jeans: Jeans are too casual for a business setting. Even if the investors you are meeting are known for their casual dress code, it's best to err on the side of caution and dress more professionally.
- Shorts: Shorts are even more casual than jeans and should be avoided when meeting with investors.
- T-shirts: T-shirts are also too casual for a business setting. If you want to wear a shirt with a graphic or logo, ensure it is professional and appropriate.
- Flip-flops or sandals: Flip-flops and sandals are too casual for a business setting. Wear dress shoes or loafers instead.
- It's also important to remember the culture of the investors you are meeting with. For example, if you are meeting with investors in Silicon Valley, you may be able to dress more casually than if you were meeting with investors in New York City. However, it's always best to err on caution and dress more professionally.

Chapter 11 Executing Successfully in Investor Meetings

11.1 Organising Roadshows

The lockdown resulted in a significant increase in first meetings happening on Zoom. While people still prefer to meet face-to-face whenever possible, video calls have become an acceptable alternative, especially in the early stages of the capital raising process. Virtual roadshows, online investor meetings, and digital platforms for outreach provide cost-effective alternatives to traditional methods.

Roadshows remain a critical part of the capital raising process for private companies. They allow companies to meet with potential investors and present their business plans in person. Roadshows can be a lot of work, but they are essential for raising capital and building investor relationships.

1. Set clear goals for your roadshow

What do you hope to achieve by hosting a roadshow? Do you want to raise a certain amount of money? Meet with a certain number of investors? Generate buzz around your company. Once you know your goals, you can start to plan your roadshow accordingly.

2. Choose the right cities

When choosing cities for your roadshow, consider the following factors:

- Do you have an anchor investor who is already interested in learning more?
- Where are your target investors located?
- Are there any industry events or conferences in the cities you consider combining with your roadshow?
- What other factors would make a city a good fit for your roadshow?

3. Identify potential investors

Once you have chosen the cities for your roadshow and your anchor meetings, you need to identify other potential investors to meet with. You can use various sources to find investors, such as online databases, industry events, and networking. When selecting investors to meet with, consider the following factors:

- Do they invest in the stage of growth that your company is in?
- Do they invest in the industry that your company is in?
- Do they have a good track record of success?

4. Create a roadshow presentation

Your roadshow presentation should be clear, concise, and persuasive. It should highlight your company's unique selling proposition, target market, competitive landscape, financial projections, and exit strategy. Be sure to practice your presentation beforehand to deliver it confidently.

5. Book meeting rooms and travel arrangements

Once you have identified potential investors and created a roadshow presentation, you must book meeting rooms and travel arrangements if you are not meeting at the investor's offices. Book your meetings well, especially if you target top investors.

6. Promote your roadshow

Let potential investors know about your roadshow in advance so that they can schedule a time to meet with you. You can promote your roadshow through email, social media, and your company website.

11.2 How to Conduct Investor Meetings

In-person investor meetings are a crucial part of the capital raising process. They allow you to connect with potential investors, answer their questions in real time, and get feedback on your business plan.

While in-person meetings can be daunting, they are also incredibly rewarding. Following the tips in this chapter can increase your chances of success and leave a positive impression on investors.

Before the meeting

- *Do your homework* - Before you meet with any investor, it's essential to do your research. This includes understanding their investment thesis, portfolio companies, and investment preferences. The more you know about the investor, the better equipped you will be to tailor your pitch and answer their questions.
- *Practice your pitch* - Your pitch is a brief overview of your company, its problem, solution, and market opportunity. Practice your pitch until it's polished and concise. You should also be prepared to answer any common questions

investors may ask.

- *Know your numbers* - Investors will want to see that you have a solid understanding of your financials. This includes your revenue, expenses, and projections. Be prepared to answer questions about your burn rate, runway, and how you plan to use the investment proceeds.
- *Prepare your materials* - Besides your pitch deck, you may want to bring other materials to your investor meeting, such as a business plan, financial model, and product demo. Be sure to print out enough copies for everyone in the room.
- *Dress professionally* - First impressions matter, so it's important to dress professionally for your investor meeting. This does not mean you must wear a suit and tie, but you should dress neatly and appropriately for the occasion.
- *Arrive early* - Arriving early for your investor meeting is always best. This shows that you are respectful of their time and that you are eager to get started. Also, it allows you to read up on any documentation about the investor at reception.

During the meeting

- *Start by building rapport* - Before you launch into your pitch, take some time to get to know the investor(s). Ask them about their background, investment interests, and what they want in a company. Ask them whether they have been busy. Complement the investor when appropriate and repeat any questions to show you are taking note of what is being said.
- *Be yourself.* Do not try to be someone you are not. Investors will appreciate your authenticity.
- *Be clear and concise in your pitch* - When it's time to give your pitch, be clear and concise. Focus on the key points of

your business plan and avoid using jargon. Be prepared to answer questions and provide more detail as needed.

- *Be enthusiastic and passionate* - Investors want to invest in people who are passionate about their businesses. Show the investor that you are excited about your company and its potential for success.
- *Be honest and transparent* - Investors can spot dishonesty from a mile away. Be open and transparent about your business, even if it means discussing your challenges.
- *Ask for the next steps* - At the end of the meeting, ask the investor for the next steps. This could involve following up with them in a week, sending them additional information, or scheduling a follow-up meeting.

Handling objections

Be prepared for tough questions. Investors will want to challenge your business plan and ensure you've considered all the potential risks. Be prepared to answer their questions honestly and confidently. No matter how well-prepared you are, investors are likely to have some objections to your business plan. This is perfectly normal. Investors are investing their hard-earned money, so they want to make sure they are making a wise decision. Reframe questions and concerns in a positive light, using persuasive language to alleviate doubts and reinforce the investment opportunity's strengths and potential.

The important thing is to be prepared to handle objections calmly and professionally. Here are a few tips:

- *Listen carefully to the objection.* Don't try to interrupt or argue with the investor. Instead, listen carefully to their objection and try to understand their point of view.

- *Acknowledge the objection.* Once you understand the objection, acknowledge it. This shows the investor that you are listening and taking their feedback seriously.
- *Address the objection directly.* Once you've acknowledged the objection, address it directly. Be prepared to provide evidence or data to support your claims.
- *If you don't have an answer, be honest.* If you don't have an answer to an investor's objection, be honest. Don't try to make up something. Instead, tell the investor that you'll look into it and get back to them.

Examples of investor objections and how to handle them

- *Your business is too risky.* Investors are naturally risk-averse but also willing to take risks on promising startups. To address this objection, highlight the potential rewards of investing in your company. Talk about the large addressable market, the strong team, and the unique value proposition. You can also mitigate the risk by asking for a smaller investment than planned.
- *Your team doesn't have enough experience.* Investors want to invest in teams with a proven track record. To address this objection, highlight the relevant experience of your team members. You can also discuss your plans to build your team as you grow.
- *Your market is too small.* Investors want to invest in companies with a large addressable market. To address this objection, talk about expanding your market reach. You can also talk about the potential for your market to grow.
- *Your valuation is too high.* Investors want to invest in companies that are fairly valued. To address this objection, be prepared to explain your valuation methodology. You can also prove that other comparable companies have been

valued at similar or higher levels.

After the meeting

- After each meeting, be sure to send a thank-you note to the investor. You can also use this opportunity to answer any questions they may have and reiterate your interest in their investment. Be persistent.
- Send a thank-you note within 24 hours of your meeting. This is a simple way to show appreciation for their time and consideration.
- If the investor requests additional information, follow up promptly. You should also follow up if you have any updates or news to share.
- Be patient - Building relationships with investors and raising capital can take time. Do not get discouraged if you do not close a deal right away. Keep following up with investors and keep pitching your company.

11.3 Speaking at Conferences

Speaking at conferences can be a great way to raise money for your company. It allows you to reach a large audience of potential investors, customers, and partners. However, choosing the right conferences to speak at and delivering your presentation in an engaging and informative format is crucial.

How to choose what conferences to speak at

- *Target audience:* Who is the conference for? Is it attended by your target investors, customers, or partners? Research the conference's history and track record. Conferences with a proven history of attracting relevant attendees and facilitating meaningful connections may offer better value for your investment.

- *Conference reputation:* Is the conference well-respected in your industry? Does it have a good track record of attracting a high-quality audience?
- *Speaking opportunities:* What speaking opportunities are available at the conference? Can you give a keynote address, a breakout session, or a panel discussion?
- *Timing and Slot Selection:* Pay attention to the timing of your speaking slot. The first day of a multi-day conference often has a higher attendance rate, as attendees are more engaged and energetic. Be mindful of scheduling, as late afternoon slots may have lower attendance.
- *Cost:* How much does it cost to speak at the conference? Is it worth the investment?

Drawbacks of conferences

- *Less personalised attention:* In a group setting, companies may receive less individual attention from investors, making it more challenging to showcase their unique value proposition and address specific investor concerns.
- *Competition for investor interest:* With multiple companies vying for attention, it can be more difficult to stand out and capture the interest of potential investors.
- *Potential for distractions:* The presence of other companies may create distractions or dilute the focus on a particular company's presentation.
- *Limited control over presentation format:* In a group setting, companies may have less control over the overall presentation format, which may not align perfectly with their specific messaging and branding.

- *Potential for unfavourable comparisons:* Investors may directly compare companies, potentially highlighting perceived weaknesses or shortcomings.

How to choose what format for your presentation

The format of your presentation will depend on the type of conference you are speaking at and the target audience. However, there are a few general tips to keep in mind.

Most people have short attention spans, so it is vital to keep your presentation concise. Aim for a presentation that is 20-30 minutes long. Use visuals, stories, and humour to engage your audience. Share valuable information with your audience that they can use to improve their businesses or lives. Tell your audience what you want them to do next: visit your website, sign up for your newsletter, or invest in your company.

Tips for choosing the suitable format for your presentation

Keynote address: Keynote addresses are typically 30-60 minutes long and are given to the entire conference audience. They are a great way to share your story, company vision, and call to action.

Breakout session: Breakout sessions are typically 20-30 minutes long and are given to a smaller audience. They are a great way to dive deeper into a specific topic and to engage with your audience more directly.

Panel discussion: Panel discussions are typically 60-90 minutes long and involve experts discussing a specific topic. They are a great way to share perspectives and get multiple people's insights.

Tips for delivering an effective presentation

- Stand straight and speak clearly and confidently.
- Project your voice so that everyone in the room can hear you.
- Make eye contact with your audience.
- Use open gestures and use facial expressions to engage your audience.
- Pause for emphasis.
- Tell stories and use humour to keep your audience engaged.
- Practice your presentation beforehand to deliver it smoothly and confidently.

Tips for using speaking engagements to raise money

Promote your speaking engagements on social media and in your email newsletter. This will help to generate interest in your company and your presentations.

Collect contact information from audience members at your speaking engagements. This will allow you to follow up with them after the event and learn more about their interest in investing in your company.

Create a landing page on your website specifically for your speaking engagements. This page should include information about your upcoming speaking engagements and links to your presentation slides and videos.

Use your speaking engagements to generate leads for new investors. For example, you can track the people who attend your speaking engagements and contact their employers to see if they want to learn more about your company.

Networking etiquette and best practices at conferences

Maintaining proper etiquette is essential in networking, as it helps build trust and respect among peers. Here are some networking etiquette and best practices:

- *Be Respectful of Others' Time:* Value people's time by being punctual for meetings scheduled at conferences. Avoid monopolising someone's time.
- *Dress Appropriately:* Dress professionally and appropriately for the networking event. Your attire should reflect the level of formality.
- *Exchange Contact Information:* When exchanging contact information, be clear and accurate. Double-check email addresses and phone numbers to ensure accuracy.
- *Follow Up Promptly:* Send a follow-up message or email shortly after meeting someone to express appreciation and continue the conversation.
- *Use Polite and Professional Language:* Maintain a professional and courteous tone in all in-person or online communications.
- *Respect Boundaries:* Respect personal boundaries and avoid intrusive or overly personal questions. Not everyone may be comfortable discussing certain topics.
- *Offer Help Before Asking for Favors:* Prioritise giving before receiving. Offer assistance or support to others in your network without expecting immediate reciprocation.
- *Be Mindful of Body Language:* Pay attention to your body language, as it conveys your attitude and intentions. Maintain good eye contact, use open body language, and offer a firm handshake.

- *Be a Gracious Host:* If you host an event or gathering, introduce people, facilitate conversations, and create a welcoming atmosphere.
- *Stay Informed and Prepared:* Stay informed about industry trends and current events to engage in meaningful conversations. Be prepared to discuss your background, interests, and goals.

11.4 Media Coverage

Media coverage can be a powerful tool for CEOs who are raising money. It can help to generate awareness for your company, attract investors, and build trust with potential customers and partners.

Investors want to invest in companies that are getting attention and have the potential to be successful. Media coverage can help to demonstrate that your company has a strong team, a viable product or service, and a large addressable market. Media coverage can also help to build trust with potential customers and partners. When people see your company in the news, they are more likely to believe it is a legitimate business with a bright future. This can be especially important for early-stage companies still trying to establish themselves in the market.

There are several things that CEOs can do to increase their chances of getting media coverage. One crucial step is to identify the right journalists to target. Look for journalists who cover your industry or who have written about similar companies in the past. You must develop a compelling pitch once you have identified a few target journalists. Your pitch should be clear, concise, and newsworthy. It should explain why your company is exciting and why journalists should care about it. It would help if you also were prepared to provide journalists with additional information, such as interviews, white papers, or product demos. The more information you can provide, the more likely journalists will write about your company.

Specific tips for getting media coverage when raising money

- *Announce your capital raising round.* This is a newsworthy event that is likely to interest journalists who cover your industry. Be sure to include all the relevant details in your announcement, such as the amount of money you raised, the types of investors who participated, and how you plan to use the funds.
- *Highlight your company's milestones.* Have you recently launched a new product, expanded into a new market, or won a major award? These are all newsworthy milestones that can help you to generate media coverage.
- *Tell your company's story.* Journalists are always looking for exciting stories to tell. Take some time to develop a narrative about your company's founding, mission, and vision for the future. This story can be a great way to introduce your company to journalists and potential investors.
- *Build relationships with journalists.* Get to know journalists who cover your industry and build relationships with them. This will make them more likely to consider your pitches and write about your company when it is newsworthy.

Using media coverage to attract investors and customers

When raising money, using media coverage to your advantage is important. Be sure to share your media coverage with potential investors. This will help them to learn more about your company and its accomplishments. You can also use media coverage to generate leads for new investors. For example, you can track the journalists who write about your company and contact their editors to see if they are interested in meeting you.

Media coverage can also build trust with potential customers and partners. When people see your company in the news, they are more likely to believe it is a legitimate business with a bright future. You can use media coverage to build trust with potential customers by sharing it on your company's website and social media channels. You can also send press releases to your customers and partners whenever your company is featured in the news.

Media coverage can be a powerful tool for CEOs who are raising money. By following the tips above, you can increase your chances of getting media coverage and using it to your advantage.

Not all media coverage is created equal. Focus on targeting high-quality media outlets that have a reach of your target audience.

Do not send out the same generic pitch to every journalist. Take the time to tailor your pitch to each journalist's specific interests and beat.

When a journalist contacts you, be sure to respond promptly and professionally. Provide them with the necessary information and be willing to answer their questions.

Once your company has been featured in the news, follow up with the journalist who wrote the story. Thank them for their coverage and send any additional information they may need.

Chapter 12 Post Meeting Excellence and Adaptability

12.1 Staying Organised and Tracking Feedback

When raising money from investors, staying organised and tracking their feedback is essential. This will help you identify common themes and trends and adjust your pitch deck and business plan.

There are several different systems that you can use to track investor feedback. Here are a few popular options:

- *Spreadsheets:* Spreadsheets are a simple and inexpensive way to track investor feedback. However, they can be time-consuming to update and maintain.
- *Customer relationship management (CRM) software*: It can track all your interactions with investors, including their feedback. CRM software can also help you to segment your investors and send targeted communications.
- *Investor tracking software:* Several software programs are specifically designed for tracking investor feedback. These programs can help you track investor interest, meeting notes, and feedback from pitch decks and business plans.
- *Investment relationship management (IRM) software*: IRM software is designed to help companies manage their relationships with investors. It can track investor feedback

and other important information such as investor contact information, investment history, and portfolio holdings.

- *Investor communication platforms*: They are designed to help companies communicate with their investors. They can distribute investor presentations, financial reports, and other news and announcements. Some investor communication platforms also allow companies to collect and track investor feedback.
- *Investor data analytics platforms:* Investor data analytics platforms help companies to collect, analyse, and visualise investor data. This data can include investor feedback and other information, such as investor sentiment and trading activity. Investor data analytics platforms can be used to identify investor trends and patterns and to develop targeted investor relations strategies.

Considerations for selection of supporting software

- *Size and complexity of the investor base:* Companies with a large and complex investor base will need a system that can handle a large volume of data and provide sophisticated analytics capabilities.
- *Budget:* Investor feedback tracking systems can range in price from free to thousands of dollars per month. Companies should choose a system that fits their budget.
- *Ease of use:* The system should be easy for investors and company employees.
- *Features:* Companies should consider the specific features they need in a system, such as the ability to collect feedback from multiple sources, track investor sentiment, and generate reports.

Tracking investor feedback

No matter what system you choose, it's essential to have a consistent process for tracking and analysing investor feedback.

- *Qualify your investors.* Not all investors are created equal. Some investors are more likely to be serious about investing in your company than others. Before tracking their feedback, take the time to qualify your investors. This includes assessing their investment focus, experience, and track record.
- *Categorise the feedback.* Once you have collected feedback from investors, categorise it into different themes. This will help you to identify common pain points and areas where you can improve your pitch deck and business plan.
- *Prioritise the feedback.* Not all feedback is created equal. Some feedback will be more important than others. Prioritise the feedback based on its relevance to your business and the investor's credibility.
- *Respond to the feedback.* Once you have prioritised the feedback, take some time to respond to it. This will show investors that you listen to their feedback and are committed to improving your business.

Examples of how you can use investor feedback to improve your capital raising process:

- *Feedback on your pitch deck:* If investors are giving you feedback on your pitch deck, use it to improve the clarity, conciseness, and persuasiveness of your presentation.
- *Feedback on your business plan*: If investors are giving you feedback on your business plan, use it to refine your financial projections, address any potential risks, and

strengthen your value proposition.

- *Feedback on your team:* If investors are giving you feedback on your team, use it to identify any areas where you need to add or strengthen your team.

By tracking and analysing investor feedback, you can improve your pitch deck, business plan, and team and increase your chances of raising money.

Additional tips for staying organised and tracking investor feedback:

- Use a central repository for all investor feedback. This could be a CRM system, investor tracking software, or a spreadsheet.
- Create a system for tagging and categorising feedback. This will help you to identify and analyse common themes and trends quickly.
- Set aside time each week to review investor feedback. This will help you to stay on top of the feedback and to make necessary adjustments to your pitch deck, business plan, and team.
- Share investor feedback with your team. This will help to ensure that everyone on your team is aware of the feedback and that you are working together to address it.

12.2 CRM Systems

If you are serious about raising capital, a CRM system is an essential tool. Choosing the right CRM system and using it effectively can increase your chances of success. Integrate the CRM with other business systems, such as your financial and marketing automation systems. This will help you streamline your capital raising process and get a complete view of your investor relationships and deal pipeline.

When choosing a CRM system for capital raising, consider your specific needs. Some of the factors to consider include the size and complexity of your investor network, the types of deals you track, your budget and your technical expertise. Choose a CRM system that is easy to use, and that integrates with your other business systems.

A CRM system can help you streamline your capital raising process by automating investor outreach, deal tracking, and reporting tasks. It can give you a real-time view of your investor relationships and deal pipeline. This information can help you to make better decisions about your capital raising strategy. A CRM system can help you to collaborate more effectively with your team members and investors. This can help you to close deals faster and more efficiently.

CRM implementation can be complex, and organisations may encounter various challenges. Communicate the benefits of CRM to employees and involve them in the decision-making process. Provide training and support to ease the transition. Establish data quality standards, regularly audit and clean the database, and implement data validation rules to maintain data accuracy. Encourage and incentivise employees to use the CRM system consistently. Highlight the positive impact on their work. Define clear and measurable CRM goals at the outset and regularly assess progress. Prioritise data privacy and compliance by following best practices and staying updated on relevant regulations.

12.3 Be Prepared for Emotional Rollercoaster

Capital raising is a critical part of business growth and expansion, but it can also be an incredibly emotional experience. CEOs of private companies face unique challenges in the capital raising process, as they often have less access to capital than public companies and may have to go through more capital raising rounds.

Founders and entrepreneurs often put their heart and soul into their businesses, and the success or failure of a capital raise can feel like a personal validation or rejection. It is essential for CEOs of private companies to be aware of the common emotions that they may experience during the capital raising process and to develop coping mechanisms for dealing with them.

Common emotions

Here are some of the common emotions that CEOs of private companies experience during the capital raising process:

- *Overconfidence:* In the early stages of the process, CEOs may feel confident about their business and their chances of raising capital. They may start to make unrealistic promises to investors and overestimate their company's value.
- *Self-doubt:* CEOs may start to doubt themselves and their business as the process progresses. They may second-guess their strategy, their pitch, and even their ability to succeed.
- *Rejection:* Many CEOs experience rejection during the capital raising process. Investors may turn them down for various reasons, including a lack of traction, unrealistic

valuation, or lack of interest.

- *Fear:* Rejection can lead to fear and anxiety, especially if the CEO has already invested a lot of time and money into their business. They may worry about running out of money or failing to achieve their goals.
- *Hopelessness:* If a CEO experiences multiple rejections, they may feel hopeless and lose faith in their business. They may even consider giving up altogether.
- *Losing patience:* CEOs sometimes can lose their temper as they face endless questioning from investors.
- *Blame game:* A blame game often starts when an investor pulls out. The CEO may blame the investor for never really having been interested. Instead, he should analyse what may have put the investor off and how to rectify the situation or do better next time.
- *Excitement:* When a CEO does the first meetings with investors, there is the excitement of seeing investors taking an interest. When the first offer comes in, there is excitement, and then when the deal closes, there is

Coping mechanisms

It is important to remember that rejection is a normal part of the capital raising process. Even the best businesses get turned down by investors from time to time. Learn from mistakes and continue to improve.

Make sure that you have a clear and concise pitch that highlights the key strengths of your business. Practice your pitch in front of a mirror or with friends and family to get feedback.

Develop a list of talking points. Identify the most common investor concerns and develop talking points to address them. This will help you feel more prepared and confident when meeting with investors.

Surround yourself with a support system. Talk to other CEOs who have been through the capital raising process. They can offer valuable advice and support.

Make sure to get enough sleep, eat healthy foods, and exercise regularly. Being physically and emotionally healthy during the capital raising process is important.

12.4 Handling Objections

Questions are always positive, as it means the investor takes your proposal seriously. Investors may have various reasons for not investing in a particular business. Here are some common objections and suggestions on how to handle them:

Market Risk
- Objection: The investor is not convinced about the market potential or sees it as too risky.
- Handling: Provide additional market research and data to support your market size and growth projections. Showcase any early traction or customer validation that demonstrates market demand.

Technical Risk
- Objection: Investors may be concerned about the technical feasibility of the startup's product or service. This is especially true for businesses in deep tech industries.
- Handling: Businesses can address this objection by providing investors with a detailed technical roadmap and explaining how they plan to overcome technical challenges. Businesses can also consider bringing on advisors or team members with deep technical expertise.

Intellectual Property Concerns

- Objection: Investors may be concerned about the startup's intellectual property portfolio. They may want to know if the startup has the necessary patents, trademarks, and copyrights to protect its innovations.
- Handling: Businesses can address this objection by providing investors with a detailed intellectual property overview. This should include a list of all intellectual property assets and the status of any pending applications. Businesses should also explain how they plan to protect their intellectual property from infringement.

Team Concerns

- Objection: Lack of confidence in the team's ability to execute the business plan.
- Handling: Emphasize the strengths and expertise of your team. Highlight relevant experience, achievements, and any industry recognition. Consider bringing on advisors or team members with complementary skills.

Team Compensation

- Objection: Investors may be concerned about the startup's team compensation structure. They may want to know if the startup offers competitive salaries and equity packages.
- Handling: Businesses can address this objection by explaining their team compensation philosophy and benchmarking salaries and equity packages against similar companies. Businesses should also be prepared to discuss their plans for future team growth and how they will ensure that their compensation structure remains competitive.

Valuation Discrepancy

- Objection: Investors may find the valuation too high or not

justified.
- Handling: Be prepared to justify your valuation with a detailed breakdown of financial projections, market comparables, and industry benchmarks. Be open to negotiation and flexible on terms.

Competitive Landscape
- Objection: Concerns about the competitive environment and differentiation.
- Handling: Clearly articulate your unique value proposition and competitive advantages. Demonstrate how your product or service stands out and why customers choose you over alternatives.

Insufficient Traction
- Objection: Lack of significant customer traction or user adoption.
- Handling: Showcase any early adopters, testimonials, or success stories. Provide a detailed plan for customer acquisition and growth. Demonstrate how the investment will accelerate traction.

Financial Performance
- Objection: Investors may be dissatisfied with financial projections or current financial performance.
- Handling: Review and refine your financial model. Provide realistic and conservative projections and explain the assumptions behind them. If possible, highlight any positive financial indicators or milestones achieved.

Regulatory Risk

- Objection: Investors may be concerned about the regulatory environment in which the business operates. This can be a particular issue for startups in emerging markets or heavily regulated industries.
- Handling: Investors will want to see that the business thoroughly understands the regulatory landscape and has taken steps to mitigate any regulatory risks. Businesses can address this by providing investors with a detailed regulatory analysis and explaining how they plan to comply with all applicable regulations.

Execution Risks

- Objection: Investors worry about the ability to execute the business plan.
- Handling: Showcase your execution strategy and milestones achieved so far. Provide a clear roadmap for how you plan to overcome challenges and mitigate risks. Demonstrate adaptability and resilience in the face of obstacles.

Exit Strategy

- Objection: Investors may be concerned about the lack of a clear exit strategy.
- Handling: Outline potential exit scenarios, whether through acquisition, IPO, or other strategic opportunities. Highlight successful exits of similar companies in the industry.

Exit Timeline

- Objection: Investors may be concerned about the exit timeline for the business. They may want to know how long they expect to wait before realising their investment.
- Handling: Businesses can address this objection by providing investors with a realistic exit timeline. This should be based

on the business model, industry trends, and comparable exits of similar companies. Businesses should also be prepared to discuss contingency plans if the exit timeline is extended.

Communication and Transparency
- Objection: Investors may feel there is a lack of transparency or communication.
- Handling: Foster open communication, providing regular updates on milestones and challenges. Address any concerns proactively and be transparent about your progress.

Macro-Economic Factors
- Objection: External economic conditions may be a concern.
- Handling: Acknowledge the concern and emphasise how your business is positioned to navigate economic challenges. Showcase any resilience or adaptability measures in your business model.

Handling objections is an ongoing process. Actively seek feedback from investors, continuously refine your pitch, and be prepared to adapt your strategy based on the concerns raised.

Chapter 13 What Can Go Wrong - 36 Pitching Pitfalls

A lot can go wrong during the capital raising process. This is a list of the top 36 common mistakes.

1. **Not being prepared**
*   This is one of the most common mistakes companies make when pitching to investors. It can manifest in several ways, such as not having a clear and concise pitch deck, being unable to answer investors' questions, and not knowing your audience.
*   A well-prepared pitch deck should be no more than 10-12 slides long and clearly articulate your company's problem, solution, market, business model, team, traction, financials, and ask. Your pitch should also be tailored to the specific investors you are pitching to. Research and learn about their investment focus and interests.
*   It is also essential to be prepared to answer investors' questions. This means discussing your company in detail, including your financial projections, target market, competitive landscape, and exit strategy.
*   Finally, it is essential to know your audience. This means understanding the types of investments they make, the stage of development they prefer, and the industries they are interested in.

2. Not updating your online presence
*   Investors will often research companies online before they agree to meet with them. It is vital to have a solid online

presence that showcases your company in a positive light.

- Make sure your website is well-designed and informative. Include testimonials from customers and partners, and publish high-quality content regularly. You should also be active on social media and engage with your audience.
- Everyone in the team must update their LinkedIn profiles. Ensure all team members show they work for your company on LinkedIn and have a company e-mail address.

3. Focusing on the product or service instead of the problem it solves

- Investors are not interested in just hearing about your product or service. They want to know how your product or service will solve a real problem for people.
- When pitching to investors, focus on the problem your company solves and how your solution is better than currently available. Explain how your solution will improve people's lives and why they should care.

4. Not having a clear business model

- Investors need to understand how you plan to make money. This means having a business model in place.
- Your business model should explain how you plan to generate revenue and how you will make a profit. It should also include your cost structure and your pricing strategy.

5. Not having a strong financial model

- Your financial model should show investors how you plan to generate revenue, how much money you need to raise, and how long it will take you to become profitable.
- Your financial model should be realistic and based on sound assumptions. It should also be flexible to update it as your business grows and changes easily.

6. Not having a solid team

- Investors are betting on the team as much as they are betting on the idea. This means it is essential to have a strong team in place.

- Your team should have the experience and expertise necessary to execute your company's vision. You should also be able to show that your team is passionate about your company and its mission.

7. Not having a large enough addressable market

- Investors want to invest in companies with the potential to grow into large businesses. This means having a large enough addressable market.

- Your addressable market is the total number of potential customers for your product or service. When pitching to investors, explain how large your addressable market is and why it is growing.

- Realistic market assessments are critical to securing funding. Do not overhype either.

8. Not being able to explain why your company is different from the competition

- Investors need to understand why your company is the best investment opportunity in its space. This means articulating what makes your company different from the competition.

- Your competitive advantage could be anything from your unique technology to your team's experience. Be sure to clearly explain what makes your company special and why investors should invest in you over other companies.

9. Not being able to articulate and underplaying your company's unique value proposition

- Your unique value proposition (UVP) makes your company unique and valuable. It is the reason why customers should choose your company over the competition.
- Your UVP should be clear, concise, and easy to understand. It should also be believable and supported by evidence.

10. Not having a clear ask

- Investors need to know how much money you are raising and how you plan to use it. This means having a clear ask.
- Your ask should be reasonable and based on your company's needs. You should also be able to explain how you plan to use the money to grow your business.

11. Not following up after the pitch

- Investors are busy, so following up with them after your pitch is essential. This will keep them engaged in your company and show that you are serious about raising money.
- In your follow-up email, thank the investor for their time and reiterate your interest in their investment. You should also answer any questions and provide them with any additional information they may need.

12. Pitching to the wrong investors

- Not all investors are created equal. Some investors focus on early-stage companies, while others focus on later-stage companies. Some investors focus on specific industries, while others focus on various industries.
- Before you pitch to any investors, be sure to do your research and make sure you are pitching to investors who are a good fit for your company and stage of development.

13. Not being honest and transparent

- Investors expect entrepreneurs to be honest and transparent about their businesses. This means disclosing any red flags or potential risks.
- If you try to sugarcoat things or hide any information from investors, they

14. Not being able to handle pressure

- Pitching to investors can be a stressful experience. Be prepared to handle the pressure and stay calm and collected.
- Do not get defensive or emotional when investors ask you tough questions. Instead, answer them calmly and professionally.

15. Being too arrogant or cocky

- Investors want to invest in entrepreneurs who are confident but not arrogant. If you come across as too arrogant or cocky, it will turn investors off.
- Be confident in your company and your ability to execute your vision, but be humble enough to admit that you do not know everything.

16. Using humour inappropriately

- Humour can be a great way to connect with investors and make your pitch more memorable. However, it is important to use humour appropriately. Avoid offensive jokes,
- Using humour in your pitch can be effective, but going overboard can backfire. Too much can make you seem unprofessional or flippant.
- Do not use humour to avoid answering tough questions from investors. This will make you seem unprepared and evasive.

- Do not use humour to attack your competitors. This will make you look unprofessional and petty.
- Make sure to tailor your humour to your audience. Avoid jokes that are too inside or that they may not understand. Be careful not to offend anyone with your humour.

17. Being too desperate

- Investors can sense desperation, so it's important to project a sense of confidence and control. If you seem too desperate, investors may think that your company is a risky investment.
- Show investors that you are confident in your company and have other options if they do not choose to invest.

18. Not being able to answer basic questions about your business

- Investors will expect you to be able to answer basic questions about your business, such as your financial projections, your target market, and your competitive landscape.
- If you cannot answer these questions, it will show investors that you are unprepared and do not fully understand your business.

19. Not being able to explain your exit strategy

- Investors want to know how they will get their money back, so be prepared to explain your exit strategy. This could involve selling your company to another company, going public, or acquiring other companies.
- Whatever your exit strategy is, explain it clearly to investors and show them how it is realistic and achievable.

20. Not having a good track record

- If you have a track record of business success, it will be easier to convince investors to invest in your new venture.
- Investors are more likely to invest in entrepreneurs with a proven success track record. If you do not have a track record, be prepared to explain why investors should invest in you anyway.

21. Not being passionate about your business

- Investors want to invest in entrepreneurs who are passionate about their businesses. Why should investors be if you do not seem excited about your company?
- Show investors that you are passionate about your business and committed to making it successful.

22. Not tailoring your pitch to the investor

- When pitching to investors, it is crucial to tailor your pitch to each investor. This means understanding their investment focus, interests, and risk tolerance.
- For example, if you pitch to a venture capital firm focusing on early-stage technology companies, you must highlight your company's disruptive technology and its potential to scale quickly. On the other hand, if you are pitching to a more risk-averse angel investor, you will need to focus on your company's strong team and proven track record.

23. Not using data and metrics to support your claims

- Investors want to see data and metrics that support your claims about your company. This could include customer growth, market share, revenue growth, and product engagement metrics.

- Using data and metrics to support your claims can show investors that you are grounded in reality and deeply understand your business.

24. Not being specific about your funding needs

- Investors need to know how much money you are raising and how you plan to use it. Be specific about your funding needs and explain how the money will be used to grow your business.
- If you are vague about your funding needs, investors may think you are unprepared or do not have a clear plan for using the money.

25. Not having a follow-up plan

- Do not just pitch to investors and then disappear. Have a follow-up plan to keep investors engaged and informed about your progress.
- This could involve sending them regular updates, inviting them to demos or events, or simply keeping in touch over email or phone. Following up with investors can show them you are serious about your business and committed to its success.

26. Not asking for feedback

- Even if you do not get an investment from a particular investor, ask them for feedback on your pitch and company. This feedback can be invaluable in helping you to improve your pitch and your company.
- Investors are often happy to give feedback to entrepreneurs, so do not be afraid to ask for it.

27. Not being able to handle rejection

- Rejection is a part of the capital raising process. Do not take it personally if an investor does not invest in your company.
- Instead, focus on learning from the rejection and improving your pitch and company. The more investors you pitch to, the better you will become at it.

28. Not building relationships with investors

- Capital raising is not just about pitching to investors. It is also about building relationships with them.
- Get to know investors and learn about their interests. Attend industry events and conferences where you can meet investors. The more investors you know, the better your chances of success when raising money.

29. Not being patient

- Capital raising takes time. Do not expect to raise money overnight.
- Be patient and persistent. Keep pitching to investors and building relationships with them. Eventually, you will find the right investors for your company.

30. Not being able to show progress

- Investors want to see that you are making progress towards your goals. Be prepared to show investors how far you have come since your last pitch.
- This could involve showing them customer growth, revenue growth, or product development milestones.

31. Not being prepared to negotiate

- Investors will expect to negotiate the terms of your investment, so be prepared to do so. This means being familiar with the different types of investment deals and

being willing to compromise.
- If you are not prepared to negotiate, investors may think you are not serious about raising money.

32. Not being able to close the deal
- Once you have an investor interested in investing in your company, you need to be able to close the deal. This means negotiating the terms of the investment and getting the investor to sign on the dotted line.
- If you cannot close the deal, you have wasted your and the investor's time.

33. Not giving investors regular updates
- Once you have raised money from investors, giving them regular updates on your progress is essential. This will keep them informed and help to build trust.
- Investors want to know that their money is being used well and that their investment is on track. You can show them that you are a responsible and trustworthy entrepreneur by giving them regular updates.
- By avoiding these mistakes, you can increase your chances of success when pitching to investors.

34. Not celebrating your successes
- When you do raise money, be sure to celebrate your success. This is a significant accomplishment, and you should be proud of yourself.
- Share your success with your team, family, and friends. This will help to keep you motivated and on track to achieve your goals.

35. Not giving back to the community

- Once you have succeeded, giving back to the community is essential. This could involve mentoring other entrepreneurs, investing in other startups, or simply donating to charitable causes.
- Giving back to the community is a great way to show your appreciation for the support you have received from others and to inspire the next generation of entrepreneurs.

36. Not being prepared for the next round of funding

- If you successfully raise money, be prepared for the next round of funding. Start thinking about your funding needs early and start building relationships with investors.
- Raising money is a never-ending process, so preparing for the next round is crucial.

On top of this, circumstances can change on the investor side. The Chief Investment Officer may leave. The investor may put all new investments on hold for reasons outside your control.

Chapter 14 Understanding Investor Processes

14.1 Investors Investment Decision Making

This chapter will also discuss the factors investors consider when making investment decisions. What are the phases the investor will go through before investing? Investors consider several factors when making investment decisions, including:

- Market size and opportunity: Investors want to invest in companies with a large addressable market and a clear opportunity for growth.
- Management team: Investors want to invest in companies with solid management teams with a successful track record.
- Technology: Investors want to invest in companies developing new technologies or with a proprietary technology advantage.
- Business model: Investors want to invest in companies with a sound business model that will likely generate revenue and profits.
- Valuation: Investors want to invest in companies that are fairly valued.

14.2 Typical Investor Q&A

Investors typically ask various questions in a meeting,

depending on the stage of the company, the industry, and the investor's investment thesis. However, there are some common questions that investors are likely to ask in any meeting. Here are some of the most common questions that investors will ask in a meeting:

- What is the problem that your company solves?
- Who is your target customer?
- What is your competitive advantage?
- What is your business model?
- What is your go-to-market strategy?
- What are your financial projections?
- What is your team's experience?
- How much money are you raising?
- How will you use the proceeds from the raise?

In addition to these general questions, investors may ask more specific questions about the company's technology, product, market, or team. Examples of more specific questions that investors may ask:

- What are the key technical risks associated with your product?
- How will you acquire customers?
- What is the size of your addressable market?
- What is your burn rate?
- What is your exit strategy?

Being prepared to answer these questions in your meeting with investors is crucial. Ensure a clear and concise pitch deck addressing all these key areas.

Tips for answering investors' questions:

- Be prepared. Take the time to think about the answers to the most common questions that investors are likely to ask.
- Be honest and transparent. Do not try to sugarcoat things or hide any information from investors.
- Be concise. Investors are busy, so get to the point quickly and avoid rambling.
- Be enthusiastic. Show investors that you are passionate about your company and your vision for the future.

Additional questions that investors may ask, depending on the stage of the company

Early-stage companies
- What is your MVP?
- How have you tested your product or service?
- What is your traction so far?
- How will you use the proceeds from the raise to scale your business?
- Later-stage companies:
- What is your customer acquisition cost?
- What is your churn rate?
- What are your key performance indicators (KPIs)?
- What are your plans for international expansion?

Additional questions that investors may ask, depending on the industry

Technology companies
- What is your intellectual property portfolio?
- What are the regulatory risks associated with your product

or service?
- How will you protect your data?

Healthcare companies
- What is the reimbursement landscape for your product or service?
- What are the clinical trial requirements for your product or service?
- How will you manage the cost of care?

Financial services companies
- What are the regulatory requirements for your product or service?
- How will you manage risk?
- How will you prevent fraud?

Preparing to answer all these questions in your meeting with investors is essential. Doing so will show investors that you understand your business and the industry in which you operate.

Concluding, investors ask various questions in meetings, depending on the stage of the company, the industry, and the investor's investment thesis. However, there are some common questions that investors are likely to ask in any meeting. By being prepared to answer these questions, you can improve your chances of success in your meeting with investors and raise the capital you need to grow your business. This is only a sample of questions. You will get 100s of questions.

14.3 Investment Processes and Investment Committees

The investment process for private companies typically involves several stages, each with its purpose and set of participants. Investment committees play an important role in many of these stages, helping to ensure that investment decisions are made thoughtfully and disciplined.

Typical stages in the investment process

The following is a general overview of the typical stages in the investment process for private companies:

- *Lead sourcing and qualification.* The investment team identifies and qualifies potential investment opportunities. This may involve networking with other investors, attending industry events, and reviewing deal flow from investment banks and intermediaries.
- *Initial due diligence.* Once a potential investment opportunity has been identified, the investment team will conduct initial due diligence to learn more about the company, its business model, and its team. This may involve reviewing the company's pitch deck, financial statements, and other relevant documents.
- *Approval by investment committee:* If the investment team is interested in pursuing an investment opportunity, they will typically present the opportunity to the investment committee for approval. Typically, an analyst will prepare a memo to present to the Investment Committee for approval to start due diligence. The investment committee may review the company's pitch deck, financial statements, and

other relevant documents and may ask questions of the investment team. Ensure you have prepared the investment team for any questions the investment committee may ask.

- *Full due diligence.* If the investment committee approves an investment opportunity, the investment team will conduct full due diligence on the company. This may involve reviewing the company's legal documents, interviewing customers and partners, and performing financial and technical due diligence. They will conduct commercial due diligence and customer and supplier due diligence, assess operational and technology risks and ESG factors, evaluate the management team and employment contracts, and review legal and regulatory compliance.

- *Term sheet negotiation.* Once the investment team has completed full due diligence, they will negotiate a term sheet with the company. The term sheet will outline the key terms of the investment, such as the valuation, the type of investment, and the rights and obligations of the investors and the company.

- *Investment agreement negotiation.* The parties will negotiate a definitive investment agreement once the non-binding term sheet has been agreed upon. The investment agreement will be a legally binding contract outlining the investment terms.

- *Closing.* Once the investment agreement has been executed, the investment will close, and the investors will provide the company with the agreed-upon funding.

- *Post-investment support:* Once an investment has closed, investors typically provide the company with ongoing support to help it achieve its goals. This may include providing strategic advice, connecting the company with potential customers and partners, and helping the company raise additional capital.

- *Exit planning:* Investors and companies should consider exit planning early in the investment process. This involves developing a strategy for investors to eventually exit their investments and realise their returns. This may involve selling the company, taking it public, or recapitalising it.

Involvement of investment committees

Investment committees are typically involved in the following stages of the investment process:

- *Initial due diligence.* Investment committees may review the initial due diligence findings of the investment team and provide feedback.
- *Investment committee presentation.* Investment committees typically make the final decision on whether or not to pursue an investment opportunity.
- *Term sheet negotiation.* Investment committees may review and approve the term sheet the investment team negotiates. They may meet every week or once a month.
- *Investment agreement negotiation.* Investment committees may review and approve the definitive investment agreement negotiated by the investment team.

Why do investors have an investment committee

- *Independent oversight.* Investment committees provide independent oversight of the investment process. This helps to ensure that investment decisions are made in a thoughtful and disciplined manner.
- *Diverse perspectives.* Investment committees typically include diverse members with different backgrounds and expertise. This diversity of perspectives can help to improve

the quality of investment decisions.

- *Accountability.* Investment committees are accountable to the board of directors and the investment fund's shareholders. This helps to ensure that investment decisions are made in the best interests of the fund.

Concluding, the investment process for private companies typically involves several stages, each with its purpose and set of participants. Investment committees play an important role in many of these stages, helping to ensure that investment decisions are made thoughtfully and disciplined.

Initial contact will be the junior level at a private equity firms

When dealing with a private equity firm, junior staff handle much of the initial and preparatory work, which can lead to frustration with business owners who prefer to engage directly with decision-makers, typically the partners or senior executives of the PE firm. This dynamic can impact the process and experience of engaging with private equity in several ways:

- *Initial Screening and Analysis:* Junior staff in PE firms are often tasked with the initial screening of potential investment opportunities, conducting preliminary analyses, and preparing reports. While they play a crucial role in filtering and structuring deals, they do not have the authority or experience to make final investment decisions.
- *Communication Gap:* CEOs and business owners often prefer to discuss strategic and complex matters directly with someone who has decision-making authority. When junior staff are the primary points of contact, it can lead to a perceived communication gap where CEOs feel their strategic vision and nuances of the business are not fully

understood or conveyed to the senior partners.

- *Expertise and Experience:* Senior partners in PE firms usually have extensive experience and a deep understanding of business strategy and industry trends. CEOs often seek their insights and advice, which junior staff might not be fully equipped to provide.

- Building Rapport and Trust: Building a strong, trusting relationship is key to any business negotiation. CEOs typically prefer to build this rapport directly with the partners who will ultimately decide on the investment rather than with junior team members.

- *Efficiency and Decision Making:* Engaging directly with senior decision-makers can expedite the decision-making process. CEOs might feel that communicating through junior staff adds an unnecessary layer to the process, potentially slowing negotiations or deal closure.

- *Negotiation and Influence:* CEOs often believe that they can better negotiate terms and influence the outcome of a deal when dealing directly with senior partners, who have the authority to make concessions or tailor the terms of the investment.

To address this frustration, some PE firms might involve senior partners earlier, especially during key meetings or strategic discussions. However, it's also important for CEOs to recognise the value junior team members bring to the process, as they often conduct the thorough groundwork informing the senior partners' decisions.

14.4 Top 15 Red Flags

1. *Lack of transparency and disclosure:* Investors need to trust that the company they are investing in is honest and

transparent about its financial position, business plans, and risks. It is considered a major red flag if a company is not forthcoming with this information.

2. *Inconsistent or inaccurate financial statements:* Investors need to be able to rely on the company's financial statements to provide an accurate picture of its financial health. It is a major red flag if the financial statements are inconsistent or inaccurate.

3. *Unexplained cash flow fluctuations:* Significant fluctuations in cash flow can be a sign of underlying problems, such as fraud or mismanagement. Investors should investigate any unexplained cash flow fluctuations carefully.

4. *High debt levels:* Excessive debt can burden a company and make it more difficult to repay its obligations. Investors should carefully consider the company's debt levels before investing.

5. *Overly optimistic projections:* Companies often make projections about their future performance, but investors should be wary of overly optimistic projections unsupported by concrete evidence.

6. *Lack of a sound business plan:* A sound business plan provides a roadmap for how the company will achieve its goals. If a company does not have a well-developed business plan, it is a major red flag.

7. *Inexperienced or unqualified management team:* The management team is responsible for executing the company's business plan and making sound decisions on behalf of the company. Investors should carefully consider the experience and qualifications of the management team before investing.

8. *Poor corporate governance:* Good corporate governance practices are essential for protecting the interests of

shareholders. Investors should be wary of companies with poor corporate governance practices.

9. *History of legal or regulatory issues:* A history of legal or regulatory issues can indicate underlying problems with the company's business practices. Investors should carefully investigate any history of legal or regulatory issues before investing.

10. *Unrealistic valuation:* The valuation of a company is the price that investors are willing to pay for a share of the company. If a company's valuation is unrealistic, it is a major red flag.

11. *Unethical or illegal business practices*: Investors should avoid companies that engage in unethical or illegal business practices, such as environmental violations, labour abuses, or anti-competitive practices.

12. *Lack of intellectual property protection:* Intellectual property (IP) is a valuable asset for many companies, and investors should be wary of companies without adequate IP protection.

13. *Overreliance on a single customer or supplier:* Companies that are overly reliant on a single customer or supplier are more vulnerable to disruptions in their business. Investors should carefully consider the company's customer and supplier base before investing.

14. *Lack of competitive differentiation:* Companies must have a clear competitive advantage to succeed in today's competitive business environment. Investors should be wary of companies that lack a clear competitive differentiation.

15. *Unrealistic exit strategy:* Companies raising capital need to plan how they will exit the investment, such as through an IPO, acquisition, or secondary sale. Investors should carefully consider the company's exit strategy before investing.

14.5 Onsite Visits by Investors

Onsite visits are a critical part of the capital raising process for private companies. They allow investors to meet the team, see the product or service in action, and better understand the company's culture. Onsite visits can also be an excellent way for CEOs to build relationships with potential investors. By showing investors around your office and answering their questions, you can make a positive impression and increase your chances of raising money.

Make sure that everyone on your team is prepared for the onsite visit. Send a briefing note about the investor to the team. This means knowing their roles and responsibilities and being able to answer any questions that investors may have. Share the FAQs and make sure everyone in the team gives the same answers. Ensure that your office is clean and tidy and that your product or service is set up and ready to go. You may also want to prepare a presentation or demo for investors.

A few days before the onsite visit, send an agenda to investors. This will let them know what to expect and help the visit run smoothly. Share the

Greet investors warmly. When investors arrive, greet them warmly and introduce yourself. Make sure that everyone on your team introduces themselves as well. Give investors a tour of your office and introduce them to your team members. This is a great way to break the ice and give investors a better understanding of your company's culture. After the tour, give investors a presentation about your company. This presentation should cover your company's mission, vision, product or service, target market, competitive advantage, business model, financial projections, and exit strategy.

After your presentation, be prepared to answer

questions from investors. This is your chance to address their concerns and sell them on your vision for the company.

Be prepared to talk about your company's traction. Investors want to see that your company is making progress and that it is gaining momentum. Be honest and transparent. Investors appreciate honesty and transparency. Be prepared to answer investors' tough questions and discuss your company's challenges. Be enthusiastic. Investors are more likely to invest in companies that they believe in. Show investors that you are passionate about your company and its mission.

Investors are busy, so ensure your onsite visit is efficient and productive. Be respectful of investors' time.

After the onsite visit, send a thank-you note to investors. You can also use this opportunity to follow up on any questions they may have had and provide them with any additional information they requested.

Onsite visits are an integral part of the capital raising process for private companies. Preparing for and conducting successful onsite visits will increase your chances of raising money from investors.

Chapter 15 Closing Deals

15.1 The Rule of 12

The rule of 12 points of contact is a guideline that suggests that it takes an average of 12 meaningful interactions with a potential investor before they are ready to close a deal. This rule is based on the idea that investors need to get to know you and your company well before they are comfortable making a significant investment.

The 12 points of contact can include:

- Initial introductions and meetings: These are your first chances to make a good impression on potential investors and learn about their investment criteria.
- Follow-up emails and calls: After your initial meeting, it is essential to follow up with potential investors to keep them informed about your progress and to answer any questions they may have.
- Due diligence meetings: Potential investors will want to conduct due diligence on your company before they invest. This may involve meetings with your management team, a review of your financial statements, and site visits.
- Negotiations: Once you have reached a term sheet with a potential investor, there will be a negotiation period to finalise the terms of the investment.

- Closing: Once the terms of the investment have been finalised, there will be a closing process to complete the paperwork and transfer of funds.

15.2 Exclusivity to Complete Due Diligence

It is common practice to grant exclusivity to an investor in a capital raising process so that they can complete due diligence. This means the company agrees not to solicit other investors during exclusivity. This gives the investor the time and space to assess the company and make an informed investment decision.

The length of the exclusivity period typically ranges from 30 to 90 days. However, it can vary depending on the transaction's complexity and the investor's needs. There may be milestones built in for an extension of exclusivity. There are several reasons why granting exclusivity is beneficial for both the company and the investor.

It prevents the company from wasting time and resources pursuing multiple investors who may not be a good fit. It allows the CEO to focus on building relationships with one investor at a time, increasing the chances of a successful deal. It can help to create a sense of urgency for the investor, which can lead to a more favourable deal for the company.

It allows the investor to do their due diligence, which can be costly, without worrying about the company being snatched away by another investor. The investor can build a rapport with the company's leadership team. It can give the investor more leverage in negotiating the terms of the investment.

Of course, there are also some potential drawbacks to granting exclusivity. It may limit the company's options if the investor decides not to invest. It could pressure the company to close a deal quickly, even if it is not the best deal they could get. It could make it difficult for the company to attract other investors if the exclusivity period expires without a deal being reached.

Ultimately, whether or not to grant exclusivity is a case-by-case decision that should be made on a per-investor basis. Companies should carefully consider their own needs and the specific circumstances of the transaction before making a decision. Do proper due diligence on the investor and ensure they have the funding before granting exclusivity.

Here are some additional factors to consider when deciding whether or not to grant exclusivity:

* The reputation and track record of the investor.
* The amount of capital the investor is willing to invest.
* The terms of the investment that the investor is proposing.
* The company's own needs for capital.
* The company's willingness to take on the risk of not finding another investor if the exclusivity period expires without a deal being reached.

If you are considering granting exclusivity to an investor, it is essential to understand the risks and benefits involved clearly. You should also consult with an experienced attorney or financial advisor to ensure you make the best decision for your company.

15.3 Negotiating and Closing Deals

Once you have found interested investors, you must negotiate the terms of the investment deal. This chapter will cover the key negotiation points, such as valuation, ownership, and board representation. It would also discuss closing the deal and getting the investment money into your company. This can be a complex process, but it is essential to get the terms right. The terms of the investment deal will significantly impact your company's future, so it is important to be prepared and negotiate from a position of strength.

Prepare thoroughly and understand your worth

- Conduct extensive research on comparable companies and industry valuations to establish a realistic range for your company's worth.
- Analyse your financial projections, market positioning, and competitive advantages to articulate your company's strengths and potential.
- Anticipate investor questions and concerns and prepare well-rehearsed responses demonstrating your expertise and confidence.

Choose the right time and leverage

- Timing is critical. Avoid raising capital when your company is in a vulnerable position or when market conditions are unfavourable.
- Assess your negotiating leverage. If investors are eager to invest, you have more bargaining power. Conversely, if there are multiple competing offers, you can play off investors.
- Consider alternative funding options if investors are not offering favourable terms.

Tips for negotiating valuation with investors

- *Be prepared to walk away.* If investors are unwilling to meet your valuation, be ready to leave the deal. Other investors out there may be willing to pay your asking price.

- *Be flexible.* Be willing to compromise on some things, such as the terms of the investment or the percentage of equity you are willing to give up.
- *Focus on the value that your company can create for investors.* Remind investors of the potential upside of your company and how they can benefit from investing in your business.

15.4 Key Legal Documents

Term Sheet

A term sheet is a *non-binding* document outlining a proposed investment's key terms and conditions. The term sheet is typically negotiated between the private company and the potential investor(s) before the parties enter a definitive investment agreement. The term sheet should include the following information:

- The type of investment (e.g., equity, debt)
- The amount of the investment
- The price per share (for equity investments)
- The conversion rate (for convertible debt investments)
- The liquidation preference (for preferred stock investments)
- The voting rights of the investor(s)
- The board representation of the investor(s)
- The pre-money valuation of the private company
- The closing date

Key points to negotiate

The term sheet is a foundational document that outlines the

key terms and conditions of the proposed investment, serving as a roadmap for the subsequent negotiation of a funding agreement. The following are some of the points to negotiate:

- Pre-money valuation and Investment Amount: The valuation of your company is the price investors are willing to pay for a stake in your company. Several factors, including the size of your market, growth potential, and competitive landscape, determine the valuation.
- Ownership: The ownership structure of your company determines who owns what percentage of the company. This is a critical negotiation point, as it will affect your control over the company and your potential financial upside.
- Investor Rights: This covers rights and privileges granted to the investors, such as voting rights, board representation and protective provisions. Investors typically want representation on your company's board of directors as it gives them a say in your company's strategic direction and allows them to monitor their investment. Circumstances under which investors have the right to veto are determined.
- Right of First Refusal: Defines conditions under which existing shareholders can purchase the shares offered to external investors.
- Pre-emptive Rights: Outline the right of existing shareholders to maintain their ownership percentage by purchasing additional shares in future rounds.
- Anti-Dilution Provisions: Protect the investor's ownership percentage.
- Information Rights: Specifies the financial and operational information the company must provide investors.
- Use of Proceeds: It will describe how the funds will be used.

- Liquidation preferences: Liquidation preferences determine how investors' investments are paid back if your company is liquidated. Investors will typically want a high liquidation preference so that they are paid back before other shareholders.
- Conversion rights: Investors may want to have the right to convert their investment into equity later. This allows them to buy more shares in your company if it is successful.
- Liquidation and Exit Preference: This defines the strategies and conditions for exit and how proceeds will be distributed in the event of a sale or liquidation of the company.
- Tag-along rights: Tag-along rights give investors the right to sell their shares if you sell them. This gives investors some protection if you decide to sell your company.
- Drag-along rights: Drag-along rights give you the right to force investors to sell their shares if you sell them. This gives you more control over the exit process.
- Conditions Precedent and Covenants: Conditions that must be met before the investment is finalised and ongoing covenants and commitments related to the investment.

Investment Agreement

An investment agreement is a legally binding contract that formalises the terms and conditions of an investment. It is a more detailed document than a term sheet and covers aspects such as the rights and obligations of investors and the company receiving the investment funds. This agreement includes clauses related to share issuance, capital contributions, use of funds, management control, warranties, representations, and other provisions necessary to protect the interests of both parties.

The investment agreement should include all the

information that was included in the term sheet, as well as additional provisions such as:

- Representations and warranties from the private company and the investor(s)
- Covenants from the private company and the investor(s)
- Conditions to closing
- Closing procedures
- Dispute resolution provisions

Shareholder Agreement

A shareholder agreement is a contract between the shareholders of a private company. It sets out the rights and obligations of each shareholder, outlines how decisions will be made within the company, and addresses issues like voting rights, management roles, dispute resolution mechanisms, transfer of shares, and restrictions on share sales. A shareholder agreement helps protect the shareholders' interests and ensures the company's smooth operation.

Other Legal Documents

In addition to the term sheet, investment agreement, and shareholder agreement, several other legal documents may be involved in the capital raising process, depending on the specific circumstances of the investment. These documents may include:

- Stock purchase agreement
- Option agreement
- Convertible note agreement
- Registration rights agreement
- Right of first refusal agreement
- Non-disclosure agreement

Negotiation tips

- Do your research: Before you start negotiating, it is essential to do your research and understand the terms that other companies in your industry have negotiated. This will give you a good starting point for negotiations.
- Be prepared to walk away: If you are unhappy with the terms, walk away from negotiations. This will show investors that you are serious about getting a good deal.
- Get everything in writing: Once you have reached an agreement with investors, get everything in writing. This will protect you if there is a dispute down the road.
- Be responsive: Investors are busy, so respond to their requests. This will show them that you are serious about closing the deal.
- Be professional: Be professional throughout the closing process. This includes being punctual, being organised, and being prepared.
- Be patient: Closing investment deals can take time. Be patient, and do not get discouraged if the process does not go as quickly as you would like.
- Get legal advice: Have an attorney review the investment documents before you sign them. This will help you understand the deal's terms and ensure that your interests are protected.
- Do not be afraid to negotiate: Investors expect CEOs to negotiate. Do not be scared to push for better terms.
- Build relationships: It is essential to build relationships with investors. This will make the negotiation process smoother and will increase your chances of success in the long run.

Closing the deal

You must close the deal once you have negotiated the investment deal terms. This involves signing the necessary legal documents and transferring the investment money into your company's bank account.

Express your gratitude to investors for their time, support, and belief in your company. Acknowledge their contributions and recognise their role in your success.

15.5 Why Investors Pull Out

There are several reasons why investors may pull out of a deal at the last minute. Some of the most common reasons include:

- *Market conditions.* If market conditions change significantly between the time an investor commits to an investment and when the investment is scheduled to close, the investor may pull out of the deal. For example, investors may be less likely to invest in risky assets such as private companies if the stock market crashes or the economy enters a recession.
- *Due diligence findings.* If the investor's due diligence process reveals new information about the company that makes the investment less attractive, the investor may pull out of the deal. For example, the investor may find that the company has undisclosed liabilities, that its management team is inexperienced, or that its product or service is not as viable as the company had claimed.
- *Competitive pressure.* If another investor offers the company better terms, the original investor may pull out of the deal. This is especially likely to happen if the company

raises money in a competitive round of funding.

- *Investor-founder mismatch*. If the investor and the company's founders have different visions for the company's future, the investor may pull out of the deal. This can happen for various reasons, such as disagreement over the company's strategy, target market, or valuation.
- *Internal changes at the investor firm:* Internal changes at the investor firm, such as a change in leadership or investment strategy, can also lead to investors pulling out of deals. For example, if a new investment committee is formed, the committee may not be as supportive of a particular deal as the old committee was.
- *Investor remorse*. Sometimes, investors get cold feet at the last minute and pull out of deals. This can happen for various reasons, such as personal financial problems, changes in the investor's investment strategy, or simply a gut feeling that the investment is not right.

In addition to factors external to the company, several company-specific issues can lead to investors pulling out of a deal. These issues can include:

- *Management turnover:* If a key member of the company's management team leaves, investors may lose confidence in the company's ability to execute its business plan.
- *Financial performance:* If the company's financial performance deteriorates, investors may no longer believe that the company is a good investment.
- *Legal or compliance issues:* If the company is involved in a legal or compliance issue, investors may become concerned about the company's reputation and prospects.

- *Competitive landscape:* If the company's competitive landscape changes significantly, investors may no longer believe that the company has a viable business model.

How to reduce the risk of investors pulling out

- Be transparent and honest with investors. Investors appreciate honesty and transparency. CEOs should be upfront with investors about the company's risks, challenges, and potential rewards.
- Set realistic expectations. CEOs should ensure investors have realistic expectations about the company's growth and profitability potential. Overpromising and underdelivering are surefire ways to alienate investors and increase the risk of their pulling out of the deal.
- Be prepared to negotiate. CEOs should be prepared to negotiate the terms of the investment with investors. This may involve compromising on valuation, the type of investment, or the rights and obligations of the investors and the company.
- Build relationships with investors. CEOs should take the time to build relationships with investors. This will help to create trust and understanding and make investors less likely to pull out of the deal at the last minute.

While there is no guarantee that investors will not pull out of a deal at the last minute, CEOs can take steps to reduce the risk. CEOs can increase the chances of a successful capital raising round by being transparent and honest with investors, setting realistic expectations, being prepared to negotiate, and building relationships with investors.

Keep the introducer to the investor cc-ed on all correspondence. Often, the CEO will take the introduction and then drop the introducer. As so much can go wrong, you should make sure the introducer is cc-ed so that when you hit a roadblock with the investor, they are up to speed and can step in to massage the situation and act as a mediator.

Additional tips for CEOs to avoid last-minute investor dropouts:

- Keep investors updated on your progress. Do not wait until the last minute to tell investors about significant developments in your business. Keep them updated on your progress regularly, both good and bad.
- Be responsive to investor inquiries. Investors expect CEOs to be responsive to their inquiries. Respond to emails and phone calls promptly and professionally.
- Be flexible. Investors may want to change the terms of the investment at the last minute. Be willing to compromise if necessary.
- Have a backup plan. If an investor pulls out at the last minute, have a backup plan. This may involve reaching out to other investors or bootstrapping your business until you can raise money in the next round of funding.

Chapter 16 Investor Relations After Closing

16.1 Benefits of Investor Relations

Once you have raised capital, you must learn how to manage your investors. Investor relations (IR) is managing and maintaining relationships with investors. It is a critical function for all companies but essential for private companies.

Private companies cannot access public markets and rely on investors to provide capital. By building and maintaining strong relationships with investors, private companies can secure the funding they need to grow and succeed.

There are many benefits of investor relations for private companies. Here are a few of the most important:

1. Access to capital
One of the benefits of investor relations is that it can help private companies secure access to capital. Investors are more likely to invest in companies they have a good understanding of and trust. By building and maintaining strong relationships with investors, private companies can increase their chances of raising capital when needed.

2. Increased valuation
Investor relations can also help to increase a private company's valuation. Investors are more likely to pay a higher price for shares in a company with a strong IR program. This is because

they know that the company is well-managed and are likely to receive good communication and support from the company after they invest.

3. Reduced cost of capital
Investor relations can also help private companies reduce their cost of capital. This is because investors are more likely to offer lower interest rates and more favourable terms to companies they have a good relationship with. A lower cost of capital can save a company a significant amount of money over time.

4. Enhanced reputation
An IR program can also help to enhance a private company's reputation. Investors are more likely to invest in companies with a good reputation and that they believe are well-managed. A robust IR program can help to build and maintain a positive reputation with investors.

5. Improved corporate governance
Investor relations can also help private companies improve their corporate governance. IR professionals ensure that companies comply with all applicable disclosure and reporting requirements. By following best practices in IR, companies can improve their corporate governance and reduce the risk of regulatory issues.

6. Increased transparency
Investor relations can also help private companies to increase their transparency. This is because IR professionals are responsible for communicating with investors regularly about the company's performance and plans. By being transparent with investors, companies can build trust and increase their chances of success.

16.2 Investor Relations Plan

There are a few key things that private companies can do to build a strong investor relations program:

- *Develop a clear IR strategy.* The first step is to develop a clear IR strategy that outlines the company's goals and objectives. This strategy should be aligned with the company's overall business strategy.
- *Identify and target key investors.* Once the company has a clear IR strategy, it must identify and target key investors. This includes identifying investors interested in the company's industry and stage of development.
- *Investor Segmentation:* Not all investors are the same. Segmenting them based on factors like investment size, involvement level, and strategic importance can help customise interactions and prioritise efforts.
- *Develop a communication plan.* The company also needs to develop a communication plan that outlines how it will communicate with investors. This plan should include regular investor updates, earnings releases, and investor conferences.
- *Investor portals:* An investor portal is a website where investors can access information about your company, such as financial statements, board meeting minutes, and investor presentations.
- *Build relationships with investors.* IR is all about building and maintaining relationships with investors. This can be done by meeting with investors in person, attending industry events, and communicating with investors regularly.

16.3 Managing Investors

Once you have raised capital, you must learn how to manage your investors. This includes informing them of your company's progress, dealing with demanding investors, and exiting your investments.

Keeping investors informed

It is essential to keep your investors informed of your company's progress. This will help build trust and confidence and give investors the information they need to make informed decisions about their investment.

There are several ways to keep investors informed, including:

- *Setting Expectations:* Set and manage expectations with investors regarding communication frequency, types of updates, and performance milestones. This helps in maintaining a healthy relationship and reduces the likelihood of misunderstandings.
- *Regular updates:* Tell investors about your company's progress. This could include quarterly, financial, or updates on specific milestones.
- *One-on-one meetings:* Schedule regular one-on-one meetings with investors to discuss their concerns and answer any questions.
- *Feedback loop between the company and its investors:* Investors can provide insights, market intelligence, and strategic advice that can be instrumental in guiding the company's direction and decisions.

- *Networking and Partnerships:* Good investor relations can open doors to new business opportunities, partnerships, and even future funding sources. Investors often have extensive networks and may facilitate introductions to potential customers, partners, or additional investors.
- *Risk Management:* Effective IR can act as a risk management tool. By maintaining open communication channels with investors, private companies can preemptively address concerns and mitigate potential issues before they escalate. This can be particularly vital in navigating crises or downturns.

Dealing with difficult investors

Every CEO will have to deal with demanding investors at some point. Difficult investors may be demanding, unreasonable, or even hostile. Be transparent with the investor about the company's performance and its plans for the future.

Be calm and professional. It is essential to remain calm and professional when dealing with difficult investors. Do not get emotional or angry. Listen to their concerns. Take the time to listen to the investor's concerns. Try to understand their perspective and why they are upset.

Be willing to negotiate with the investor, but do not be afraid to stand up for yourself and your company's interests.

If you are having trouble dealing with a problematic investor, seek help from your board of directors or a professional advisor.

Additional tips for managing investors

Investors expect CEOs to be open and transparent with them. This means being truthful about the company's performance, challenges, and plans. Respond to investor inquiries promptly and professionally. Do not wait for investors to come to you with questions or concerns. Be bold and reach out to them regularly. Treat investors respectfully, even if you disagree with them. Remember that they are your partners. Investors are your partners in your business. They are investing in your company because they believe in it and you. Treat them accordingly.

Chapter 17 Exit Strategies

Eventually, you will want to exit your investments and return the money to your investors. This is known as an exit. There are several different ways to exit an investment, each with advantages and disadvantages. The best way to exit your investment depends on your company's circumstances. You should work with your board of directors and financial advisors to develop an exit plan in your company's and your investors' best interests. There are four main types of exits for private companies.

17.1 Initial Public Offering (IPO)

An IPO is when a company sells its shares to the public for the first time. This is the most prestigious type of exit but also the most complex and expensive. To go public, a company must meet stringent financial and regulatory requirements.

Advantages of an IPO
- *Raising significant capital:* An IPO can provide a company with a substantial amount of capital that can be used to fund growth initiatives, such as expanding operations, developing new products or services, or acquiring other companies. This influx of capital can significantly accelerate a company's growth trajectory and help it achieve its long-term goals.
- *Enhancing visibility and credibility:* Going public can significantly increase a company's visibility and credibility in the market. As a publicly traded company, the company's financial performance and business activities will be subject

to public scrutiny, which can enhance investor confidence and attract new customers and partners.

- *Providing liquidity for shareholders:* An IPO allows early investors and company founders to monetise their investments and realise the returns on their capital. By selling their shares on the public market, shareholders can gain liquidity and diversify their portfolios. This can be a significant benefit for investors who have been holding shares in the company for an extended period.

Disadvantages of an IPO
- *Complexity and expense:* The IPO process is complex and involves numerous steps, from selecting underwriters to preparing regulatory filings and marketing the offering to potential investors. This process can be time-consuming and costly, requiring significant financial and legal expertise.
- *Extensive disclosure requirements:* Publicly traded companies are subject to extensive disclosure requirements, including filing quarterly and annual reports with the Securities and Exchange Commission (SEC). These disclosures must provide detailed information about the company's finances, operations, and risks, which can limit the company's ability to maintain certain levels of confidentiality.
- *Ongoing regulatory obligations:* Publicly traded companies must comply with ongoing regulatory requirements, such as Sarbanes-Oxley Act (SOX) compliance and corporate governance guidelines. These regulations can be burdensome and require ongoing investment in compliance resources.

In addition to the above, it is important to consider the following factors when deciding whether or not to pursue an IPO:

- *Company's financial performance and growth prospects:* Companies with a strong track record of financial performance and promising growth prospects are more likely to raise significant capital successfully through an IPO.
- *Market conditions:* Favourable market conditions, characterised by strong investor appetite for IPOs, can increase the likelihood of a successful offering and potentially command a higher valuation for the company's shares.
- *Management team's experience and capabilities:* An experienced and capable management team is crucial for navigating the complex IPO process and ensuring the company's long-term success as a publicly traded entity.

Time to prepare an IPO and execute

The time it takes to prepare an IPO can vary significantly depending on the company's size, complexity, and regulatory requirements. However, the process can generally take six months to two years or more. Key steps involved in preparing for an IPO and their estimated timelines:

Pre-IPO Stage

- *Initial Planning and Feasibility Assessment (3-6 months):* Evaluate the company's financial readiness, growth prospects, and market fit for an IPO. Assess the company's compliance with regulatory requirements and identify gaps that must be addressed.
- *Selection of Underwriters and Legal Advisors (2-4 months):* Conduct a competitive search and select investment banks to act as underwriters and manage the IPO process. Engage legal counsel to advise on regulatory compliance, securities law, and corporate governance matters.

- *Preparation of Financial and Regulatory Filings (6-12 months):* Audit and review financial statements to ensure accuracy and compliance with accounting standards. Draft and file registration statements with the Securities and Exchange Commission (SEC), providing detailed information about the company's finances, operations, and risks. Respond to SEC comments and address any questions or concerns raised during the review process.

IPO Execution Stage
- *Roadshow and Investor Marketing (4-6 weeks):* Conduct a roadshow to present the company's investment opportunity to potential investors. Prepare marketing materials and engage with institutional investors and investment firms to generate interest in the IPO.
- *Pricing and Allocation of Shares (1-2 weeks):* Determine the initial offering price for the shares based on investor demand and market conditions. Allocate shares among institutional investors and retail investors based on subscription orders received.
- *IPO Launch and Trading (1-2 weeks):* Start trading the company's shares on a public stock exchange. Monitor market performance and respond to any issues or trading irregularities.
- Post-IPO Compliance and Reporting: Comply with ongoing SEC reporting requirements, including quarterly and annual filings. Maintain investor relations and provide regular updates on the company's performance and business activities.

17.2 Special Purpose Acquisition Companies (SPACs)

SPACs are publicly traded companies created for the sole purpose of acquiring or merging with an existing company. They have become a popular alternative to traditional IPOs for companies seeking to go public.

Advantages of SPACs

- *Speed to Market:* SPACs can often complete an acquisition or merger faster than a traditional IPO process, which benefits companies looking to access public markets quickly. It may take 4-9 months. More complex businesses might require longer due diligence and regulatory review.

- *Price Certainty:* The terms of the deal are negotiated upfront in a SPAC merger, providing price certainty not available in a traditional IPO, where pricing can be subject to market fluctuations.

- *Expertise of SPAC Management:* SPACs are typically led by experienced investors or industry experts who can provide strategic guidance and credibility to the target company.

- *Reduced Underwriting Risk:* Since SPACs raise capital before identifying a target company, the risk of underwriting is reduced compared to traditional IPOs.

- *Access to Capital:* For the target company, merging with a SPAC can provide access to capital that might not be available through private funding rounds or traditional IPOs.

- *Flexible Deal Structure:* SPAC transactions can be structured in various ways to suit the needs of the target company and the SPAC investors.

Disadvantages of SPACs

- *Dilution:* The SPAC structure often includes significant incentives for the SPAC founders, which can result in dilution for the shareholders of the target company.
- *Regulatory and Market Risks:* SPACs are subject to regulatory scrutiny, and there are concerns about the sustainability of their popularity, which could lead to market risks.
- *Pressure to Find a Target:* SPACs have a limited timeframe (usually two years) to complete a merger, which can pressure the SPAC management to make a deal, potentially leading to less favourable terms for the target company.
- *Investor Redemptions:* SPAC investors typically have the right to redeem their shares before a merger, which can lead to uncertainty regarding the amount of capital available to the target company.
- *Integration and Performance Risks:* Like any merger or acquisition, there is a risk that the integration of the SPAC and the target company may not go smoothly, or the target company may not perform as expected post-merger.
- *Reputational Risks:* The rapid increase in SPACs and some high-profile failures have led to scrutiny and scepticism, potentially affecting the reputation of companies choosing this route.

In summary, while SPACs offer an alternative pathway to going public with certain advantages like speed and expertise, they also carry risks related to dilution, regulatory challenges, and deal execution. Companies considering a SPAC merger should weigh these factors carefully against their specific circumstances and goals.

17.3 Acquisition

An acquisition, a sale by the company, is a common and often lucrative exit strategy for private companies. It involves one company purchasing another, resulting in the acquired company's assets, liabilities, and business operations being transferred to the acquiring company.

This exit strategy can be particularly attractive for companies seeking a quick and efficient way to realise the value of their investments and provide shareholders with liquidity.

Types of acquisitions

- *Friendly Acquisitions:* In a friendly acquisition, the two companies involved reach a mutual agreement on the terms of the sale. Both parties collaborate to ensure a smooth and successful transaction, often involving negotiations and due diligence processes.
- *Hostile Acquisitions:* In a hostile acquisition, one company attempts to acquire another company without the consent or cooperation of the target company's management. This type of acquisition often involves a takeover bid, where the acquiring company makes a direct offer to purchase the target company's shares at a specified price.

Advantages of acquisitions

- *Quick and Easy Exit:* Acquisitions can provide a relatively quick and straightforward path to exiting an investment compared to other options, such as an IPO, which can be lengthy and complex.

- *Premium for Shares:* In a successful acquisition, shareholders often receive a premium for their shares, meaning they receive a price higher than the current market value of their shares. This premium represents the value the acquiring company sees in the target company and its potential for future growth.
- Liquidity for Shareholders: Acquisitions allow shareholders to cash out their investment and realise the returns on their capital. This liquidity can benefit early investors or those seeking to diversify their portfolios.

Disadvantages of acquisitions

- *Potential for Unfair Pricing:* There is a risk that shareholders may not receive a fair price for their shares in an acquisition. This is particularly true in hostile acquisitions, where the acquiring company may attempt to buy the target company at a lower price than its actual worth.
- *Limited Shareholder Control:* In an acquisition, shareholders often have limited control over the terms of the sale. The companies' management teams typically handle the negotiations and decision-making process, leaving shareholders with little say in the outcome.
- *Forced Share Sales:* In some cases, shareholders may be forced to sell their shares even if they do not wish to do so. This can occur in certain types of acquisitions, such as a short-form merger or a squeeze-out merger, where minority shareholders may have their shares involuntarily converted into shares of the acquiring company.

Decision-Making Factors

The decision to pursue an acquisition as an exit strategy should be carefully considered after evaluating various factors, including:

- *Company's Financial Performance and Growth Prospects:* Companies with a strong financial track record and promising growth prospects are more likely to attract favourable acquisition offers.
- *Market Conditions:* Favourable market conditions, characterised by a strong appetite for acquisitions in the company's industry, can increase the likelihood of a successful acquisition and potentially command a higher valuation.
- *Management's Vision and Objectives:* The company's management team should carefully assess whether an acquisition aligns with the company's long-term vision and objectives.
- *Shareholder Preferences:* The company should consider the preferences of its shareholders and ensure that an acquisition is in the best interests of all stakeholders.

17.4 Secondary Sale

A secondary sale is when a company sells its shares to another investor. This can be done through a private placement or a public exchange. Private placements typically sell shares to a small group of accredited investors. Public exchanges are used to sell shares to the general public.

Advantages of a secondary sale
- A secondary sale can be a relatively quick and easy way to

exit an investment.
- Shareholders can negotiate a price for their shares.
- Shareholders can choose to sell all or part of their investment.

Disadvantages of a secondary sale
- Shareholders may not receive a fair price for their shares.
- Shareholders may have to pay a commission to a broker.
- There may be a limited market for the company's shares.

17.5 Liquidation

A liquidation is when a company sells its assets and pays back its investors. This is the least common type of exit for private companies, but it is sometimes the only option.

Liquidations can be caused by various factors, such as financial distress, management failure, or a change in the company's industry.

Advantages of a liquidation
- Shareholders can receive a return on their investment.
- Shareholders can cash out their investment.

Disadvantages of a liquidation
- Shareholders may not receive a full return on their investment.
- Shareholders may have to pay taxes on their capital gains.
- Choosing the Right Exit Strategy

17.6 Choosing the right exit strategy

The best exit strategy will depend on a variety of factors, including:

- The stage of your company's development
- The industry in which your company operates
- The financial performance of your company
- The needs and preferences of your investors

If you are trying to decide which exit strategy is right for your company, you should work with your board of directors and financial advisors to develop a plan.

- Start planning early. The earlier you start planning for your exit, the more options you will have.
- Get input from your investors. Your investors will have their preferences and expectations about your exit strategy.
- Be prepared to negotiate. You may need to negotiate the terms of your exit with potential acquirers or investors.
- Be patient. It may take some time to find the right exit strategy and to complete the exit process.

Exiting an investment can be a complex and challenging process. However, by carefully considering your company's specific circumstances and working with your board of directors and financial advisors, you can choose the right exit strategy for your company and your investors.

Chapter 18 Cyber Security Risks

There are several reasons why cybersecurity is important for capital raising. First, cybercriminals may target private companies raising capital to steal investor data or capital raising proceeds. Second, a cyberattack can disrupt a company's capital raising efforts and damage its reputation. Third, a cyberattack can lead to financial losses for the company and its investors.

Common cybersecurity risks for capital raising

- *Phishing attacks:* Phishing attacks are emails or text messages that appear to be from a legitimate source, such as a bank or investment firm. A phishing attack aims to trick the recipient into revealing sensitive information, such as their login credentials or credit card numbers.
- *Malware attacks:* Malware is malicious software that can damage or disable computer systems. Malware can be spread through email attachments, malicious websites, or USB drives.
- *Data breaches:* A data breach is an unauthorised disclosure of confidential information. Data breaches can be caused by hackers, malicious insiders, or accidental human error.
- *Denial-of-service attacks:* A denial-of-service attack makes a website or online service unavailable to its intended users. Denial-of-service attacks can be carried out by flooding the service with traffic or by exploiting vulnerabilities in the service's software.

How to protect your capital raising efforts from cyberattacks

- *Implement strong cybersecurity policies and procedures.* Cybersecurity policies and procedures should outline how the company will protect its data and systems from cyberattacks. These policies and procedures should be regularly reviewed and updated to reflect changes in the cybersecurity landscape.
- *Train employees on cybersecurity best practices.* Employees should be trained on how to identify and avoid common cybersecurity threats. This training should be conducted regularly to ensure employees know the latest cybersecurity threats.
- *Use strong passwords and multi-factor authentication.* Strong passwords and multi-factor authentication can help to protect accounts from unauthorised access.
- *Keep software up to date.* Software updates often include security patches that can help to protect against known vulnerabilities.
- *Have a backup plan.* A backup plan can help to minimise the impact of a cyberattack. The backup plan should include regularly backing up data and testing the backups to ensure they can be restored successfully.

Cybersecurity considerations for capital raising technologies

In addition to the general cybersecurity measures listed above, there are some specific cybersecurity considerations for specific capital raising technologies.

For example:

- *Crowdfunding platforms:* Crowdfunding platforms are a popular way for private companies to raise capital. However, crowdfunding platforms are also a target for cybercriminals. Private companies using crowdfunding platforms should carefully review the platform's security features and take steps to protect their investor data.
- *Online payment processors:* Online payment processors are used to process donations from online capital raising campaigns. Private companies using online payment processors should choose a reputable processor and implement strong security measures to protect their donors' credit card information.
- *CRM systems:* CRM systems are used to manage relationships with investors. Private companies using CRM systems should carefully review the system's security features and take steps to protect their investor data.

Additional tips for cybersecurity

- *Use a secure website.* Your website should be hosted on a secure server using a secure connection (HTTPS).
- *Use a firewall and intrusion detection system.* A firewall can help block unauthorised access to your network, while an intrusion detection system can help identify and respond to cyberattacks.
- *Monitor your systems for suspicious activity.* You should regularly monitor your systems for suspicious activity, such as unusual login attempts or spikes in network traffic.
- *Have a plan for responding to cyberattacks.* You should have a plan for responding to cyberattacks, such as containing the attack, notifying affected parties, and restoring your data.

Chapter 19 The Future of Capital Raising

In the past, CEOs had to rely on a small number of traditional capital raising channels, such as venture capitalists, angel investors, and banks. However, new technologies and trends create new capital raising opportunities for CEOs.

Ways that new technologies and trends are changing the future of capital raising

- *Crowdfunding platforms:* Crowdfunding has democratised capital raising by providing businesses with an alternative to traditional funding sources, allowing them to access funds from a wide pool of individual investors. This has enabled entrepreneurs to launch innovative projects and businesses that might not have been possible through traditional means. Some popular crowdfunding platforms include Kickstarter, Indiegogo, and GoFundMe.
- *Social media*: Social media connects CEOs with potential investors and builds relationships with them. CEOs can use social media to share their company's story, promote their capital raising campaign, and engage with potential investors.
- *Blockchain technology*: Blockchain technology introduces transparency, security, and immutability to the capital raising process. Blockchain-based crowdfunding platforms can automate transactions, reduce fraud, and provide real-time visibility into investment activities. This can increase trust and confidence among both investors and businesses.

- *Artificial intelligence (AI)*: AI is transforming the capital raising process by automating tasks, providing data-driven insights, and personalising the investor experience. AI can analyse vast amounts of data to identify promising investment opportunities, assess creditworthiness, and match investors with suitable projects. This can streamline the process and make it more efficient for both parties.

The convergence of these technologies can potentially create a more efficient, transparent, and data-driven capital raising ecosystem. Here are some of the specific benefits that can be expected:

- *Reduced costs:* Automation and streamlined processes can significantly reduce the administrative costs associated with capital raising.
- *Increased transparency:* Blockchain technology can provide real-time visibility into investment activities, reducing the risk of fraud and increasing investor confidence.
- *Improved risk assessment:* AI algorithms can analyse vast amounts of data to assess creditworthiness and identify potential risks, helping investors make informed decisions.
- *Personalised investor experience*: AI can be used to personalise the investor experience, providing them with tailored recommendations and insights based on their risk tolerance and investment goals.
- *Access to new investment opportunities:* Blockchain technology can facilitate cross-border transactions and enable businesses to raise capital from a global pool of investors, opening up new opportunities for growth and expansion.

The convergence of crowdfunding, blockchain, and AI is still in its early stages, but it can revolutionise how businesses raise capital and investors make investment decisions. As these technologies continue to develop, we expect to see even more innovative and efficient capital raising solutions emerge.

CEOs can prepare for the future of capital raising

- *Building a strong online presence*: CEOs should build an online presence for their company. This includes creating a website, being active on social media, and producing high-quality content. An online presence will help CEOs to connect with potential investors and to build relationships with them.
- *Educating themselves about new technologies and trends:* CEOs should learn about new technologies and trends that are changing the capital raising landscape. This will help to identify new capital raising opportunities and to avoid potential pitfalls.
- *Using the right tools and platforms:* CEOs should use the right tools and platforms to raise capital. This may include crowdfunding platforms, blockchain-based investment vehicles, and AI-powered capital raising tools.

Chapter 20 Crowd Funding: Democratising Capital Raising

The rise of crowdfunding platforms

Crowdfunding has emerged as a revolutionary approach to capital raising, democratising the process and providing entrepreneurs and businesses with an alternative to traditional funding sources. Crowdfunding platforms have increased in recent years, offering diverse options for businesses seeking to raise capital from a wide pool of individual investors.

Types of crowdfunding

There are several types of crowdfunding, each with unique characteristics and features. Some of the most common types of crowdfunding include:

- *Reward-based crowdfunding:* In reward-based crowdfunding, businesses offer backers rewards for their investment. These rewards can range from simple thank-you notes to exclusive products or services.

- *Equity crowdfunding*: In equity crowdfunding, backers invest in a company in exchange for a share of ownership. This type of crowdfunding allows businesses to raise larger amounts of capital and gives backers a stake in the company's future success.

- *Debt crowdfunding*: In debt crowdfunding, backers lend money to a company in exchange for regular interest payments. This crowdfunding type is similar to traditional bank loans but often offers more flexibility and lower interest rates.

- *Niche crowdfunding*:   There has been a rise in niche crowdfunding platforms that cater to specific industries, interests, or types of projects.

Benefits and challenges of crowdfunding

- *Access to a broader pool of investors*: Crowdfunding platforms allow businesses to reach a wider pool of potential investors than traditional methods, including individuals who may not have been able to invest in the past.
- *Reduced costs:* Crowdfunding can be a more cost-effective way to raise capital than traditional methods, as it eliminates the need for intermediaries and expensive marketing campaigns.
- *Increased brand awareness:* Crowdfunding campaigns can help businesses generate buzz and increase brand awareness, even if they are not fully funded.
- *Validation:* Crowdfunding can be used not just to raise funds but also to test the market viability of a product or concept, gather feedback, and validate ideas before full-scale production.

Challenges

- *Competition:* The crowdfunding landscape is becoming increasingly competitive, making it difficult for businesses to stand out.
- *Regulatory hurdles:* Crowdfunding is subject to various regulations, which can complicate the process.
- *Investor expectations:* Crowdfunding backers can have high expectations, and businesses need to be prepared to deliver on their promises to maintain their reputation and attract future funding.

Success not guaranteed

Understanding the success rates of crowdfunding campaigns can help set realistic expectations for businesses. The average success rate is lower than 25%. The average crowdfunding campaign raises about $28,000. The average number of backers for crowdfunding projects is around 45, emphasising the community-driven nature of crowdfunding. Different platforms have varied success rates, influenced by their models and the types of crowdfunding they support. In 2020 alone, there were over six million crowdfunding campaigns worldwide. The market is expected to grow exponentially, potentially reaching $300 billion by 2030.

Sectors best suited to crowdfunding

Certain sectors have shown to be more amenable to crowdfunding than others. Notably, platforms like Kickstarter and Indiegogo have seen considerable success in specific areas:

- *Technology and Innovative Concepts:* Platforms like Kickstarter are particularly well-suited for innovative technology projects. The data indicates that tech projects have successfully raised significant funding on such platforms, suggesting a strong interest from backers in supporting innovative tech ventures.
- *Food and Beverage:* The food and beverage sector leads in equity crowdfunding, as observed on platforms like WeFunder. This might be due to the universal appeal and tangible nature of food and beverage products, which can draw a wide range of investors.
- *Social Causes:* Platforms like GoFundMe have become increasingly popular for raising funds for social causes, including medical expenses, disaster recovery, and community projects. This trend reflects a growing desire

among individuals to contribute directly to causes they care about.

- *Games:* The gaming sector, including video games and tabletop games, has also seen significant success in crowdfunding. Platforms like Kickstarter have been particularly effective for game developers to raise funds, demonstrating the strong community support within the gaming industry.

The success in these sectors is likely due to a combination of factors, including the tangible nature of the products, the passion of the consumer base, and the ability of these projects to capture the imagination of potential backers. Moreover, the rise of niche crowdfunding platforms catering to specific sectors such as real estate, environmental projects, or social causes further facilitates the success of crowdfunding in these areas by reaching more targeted audiences. These trends suggest that sectors with a strong community appeal, tangible products, or innovative concepts are more likely to succeed in crowdfunding campaigns.

Chapter 21 How to Use Social Media

21.1 Best Practices

In the digital age, leveraging the power of social media has become an integral component of the capital raising process for CEOs and entrepreneurs. Social media platforms offer a unique opportunity to connect with a global audience, engage with potential investors, and build brand awareness.

This chapter will explore the best practices and strategies for effectively using social media in your capital raising efforts.

If you are a CEO considering using social media for capital raising, here are a few tips:

- *Platform Selection*: Not all social media platforms are equal. Some platforms like LinkedIn, YouTube and Twitter (rebranded X) are better suited for professional networking and connecting with potential investors. Platforms like Facebook, Instagram and TikTok are better suited for building brand awareness and engaging customers.
- *Audience Segmentation*: Consider your target audience when choosing platforms. Different investors may frequent various social media sites. Tailor your content to match the demographics and preferences of your chosen platform.
- *Profile Optimization:* Ensure your social media profiles are complete and professional. Use high-quality photos and videos and write engaging captions.

- *Engaging Content:* Craft engaging and authentic content that resonates with your audience. The role of compelling captions, storytelling, and visual elements in capturing attention.
- *Consistency and Scheduling*: Establish a regular posting schedule to maintain a consistent online presence. Use scheduling tools to plan and automate posts, ensuring a steady flow of content.
- *Storytelling:* Use social media to tell your company's story and its mission. Highlight your company's strengths and accomplishments.
- *Strategic Promotion:* Craft a targeted and strategic plan for promoting your capital raising campaign on social media. Develop a content calendar that includes campaign updates, announcements, and milestones.
- *Engage with potential investors:* Respond to comments and questions from potential investors promptly and professionally. Encourage engagement with your campaign by creating interactive content, such as polls, Q&A sessions, or live streams. Leverage user-generated content and user testimonials to build trust and credibility.
- *Direct Messaging:* Use direct messaging on platforms like LinkedIn to establish one-on-one connections with interested investors. Personalise your outreach and provide additional information as needed.
- *Use social media analytics:* Track your social media analytics to see what content resonates with your audience and what does not. Adjust your social media strategy accordingly.

Additional tips

- *Use relevant hashtags*: Hashtags are a great way to get your content seen by more people. When you use relevant hashtags, your posts will show up in search results for those hashtags.

- *Run social media ads:* Social media ads can be a great way to reach a targeted audience and promote your capital raising campaign.
- *Work with influencers:* Collaborate with industry influencers to expand your reach and generate interest in your capital raising campaign. Leverage the credibility and audience of influencers to endorse your venture.
- *Be transparent:* Be transparent and honest with potential investors about your company and its capital raising campaign.
- *Be patient:* It takes time to build relationships with potential investors and to raise capital.

Social media is a powerful tool that can transform the capital raising process. With the right platform choices, engaging content, and strategic planning, CEOs can effectively reach a global audience of potential investors, create meaningful connections, and promote their capital raising campaign.

However, it's crucial to be mindful of the time commitment, privacy considerations, and ethical practices when leveraging social media for capital raising. By implementing the strategies outlined in this chapter, CEOs can harness the full potential of social media in their capital raising endeavours.

21.2 How to Use LinkedIn

LinkedIn is a powerful tool for raising capital, allowing you to connect with potential investors directly. Here are some tips on how to use LinkedIn to connect with potential investors:

- *Optimize your LinkedIn profile.* Make sure your LinkedIn

profile is complete and up-to-date and that it highlights your relevant experience and expertise. Be sure to include keywords that investors are likely to search for. Please make sure everyone in your team has also updated their LinkedIn profile, otherwise, it may look like they are either not full-time or not committed to your business.

- *Join relevant LinkedIn groups.* There are several LinkedIn groups dedicated to capital raising and investing. Joining these groups will give you access to a network of potential investors and allow you to share your investment pitch with a broader audience.
- *Connect with individual investors.* Once you have identified potential investors, contact them and connect with them on LinkedIn. When sending a connection request, personalise your message and explain why you are interested in joining.
- *Engage with potential investors.* Once you are connected with potential investors, engage with them by liking and commenting on their posts and sharing your content. This will help you to build relationships with potential investors and stay top-of-mind.
- *Send direct messages to potential investors.* Once you have established a relationship with a potential investor, you can send them a direct message to introduce yourself and your investment opportunity. Keep your message concise and to the point, and include a link to your pitch deck.

Tips for connecting with potential investors on LinkedIn

- *Use LinkedIn Sales Navigator.* LinkedIn Sales Navigator is a premium tool that gives you more detailed information about potential investors, such as their job titles, investment interests, and contact information.
- *Use LinkedIn Recruiter.* LinkedIn Recruiter is a premium tool

that allows you to search for and contact potential investors directly.

- *Use third-party tools.* Several third-party tools can help you to find and connect with potential investors on LinkedIn. Some popular tools include LeadConnect and ProspectIn.

Connecting with potential investors on LinkedIn is the first step in the capital raising process. You must then build relationships and convince them to invest in your company. This can be a time-consuming process. After you have connected with an investor on LinkedIn, you move the conversation to email.

Tips for building relationships with potential investors

- Be responsive to their messages and requests.
- Be transparent and honest about your company and your investment opportunity.
- Be patient and persistent. Building relationships with potential investors and convincing them to invest in your company may take some time.

21.3 How to Use Twitter (rebranded X)

Tips on how to use X for capital raising:

- *Create a strong X profile.* Your X profile is your first impression on potential investors. Make sure it is complete and up-to-date and that it highlights your relevant experience and expertise. Be sure to include keywords that investors are likely to search for.
- *Follow the right people.* Follow potential investors, industry experts, and other relevant accounts on X. This will help you

stay up-to-date on your industry's latest news and trends and allow you to interact with potential investors.

- *Share your investment pitch.* X is a great platform to share your investment pitch with potential investors. When writing your pitch, be clear and concise, and focus on the key benefits of your investment opportunity. Be sure to include a link to your pitch deck in your tweet.
- *Engage with potential investors.* Retweet their tweets, comment on their posts, and ask them questions. This will help you build relationships with potential investors and stay top-of-mind.
- *Use relevant hashtags.* Hashtags are a great way to reach a broader audience on X. When tweeting about your capital raise, use relevant hashtags such as "#capitalraising," "#venturecapital," and "#angelinvestor."

How to generate publicity for your capital raise on X

- *Announce your capital raise.* Use X to announce your capital raise to your followers and the broader X community. Be sure to include information about your investment opportunities, such as the amount of capital you are raising, the stage of your company, and your industry.
- *Share news and updates.* Use X to share news and updates about your company and your capital raise. This could include news about new partnerships, product launches, or awards. Be sure to include relevant hashtags in your tweets.
- *Run X contests.* X contests are terrific for generating excitement and engagement around your capital raise. You could offer prizes such as free products or services or even the opportunity to invest in your company. Use relevant hashtags and promote your contest on other social media platforms.

- *Partner with influencers.* Partner with influencers in your industry to help you generate publicity for your capital raise. Influencers can help you to reach a wider audience and to build credibility for your investment opportunity.

Here are some additional tips for using X for capital raising

- *Be consistent.* Tweet regularly and consistently about your capital raise. This will help you to stay top-of-mind with potential investors.
- *Be authentic.* Be yourself and be genuine in your interactions with potential investors.
- *Be transparent.* Be honest and upfront about your investment opportunity.
- *Be patient.* It takes time to build relationships with potential investors and to generate publicity for your capital raise. Don't get discouraged if you don't see results immediately.

21.4 Regulatory Constraints on Social Media

Social media and influencers can be potent allies in the dynamic world of private company capital raising. However, CEOs must navigate this landscape keenly, aware of the risks involved.

By understanding the regulatory constraints, embracing best practices, and fostering a culture of compliance within their organisations, CEOs can harness the power of social media and influencers while mitigating potential pitfalls.

As we tread this fine line between innovation and regulation, it is the responsibility of CEOs to lead their companies with prudence and foresight, ensuring that the allure of social media does not overshadow the imperative of legal and ethical capital raising practices.

1. SEC Regulations
- Allowed: General solicitations on social media are permissible for Regulation D offerings, but companies must take measures to verify accredited investor status.
- Caution: Avoid making false or misleading statements and ensure compliance with Regulation FD (Fair Disclosure).

2. Anti-Fraud Provisions
- Allowed: Companies can use social media to disseminate factual information about the business.
- Caution: Misleading statements, intentional omissions, or false claims are strictly prohibited under anti-fraud provisions.

3. Quiet Period Restrictions
- Allowed: Companies can continue to use social media during a capital raising 'quiet period' but must avoid discussing specific aspects of the offering.
- Caution: Detailed discussions about the offering terms or potential investors should be avoided during this period.

4. Testimonials and Endorsements
- Allowed: Companies can share positive testimonials and endorsements, but they must be genuine and not misleading.
- Caution: False or exaggerated endorsements may violate SEC regulations.

5. Social Media Disclosures
- Allowed: Companies must include required disclaimers and disclosures in their social media communications.

- Caution: Failure to include necessary disclosures may lead to regulatory scrutiny.

Chapter 22 The Impact of Blockchain

Blockchain technology is one of the most transformative technological innovations in recent years. Beyond its association with cryptocurrencies like Bitcoin, blockchain offers many possibilities in finance and investment. In this chapter, we embark on a journey to explore how blockchain technology is revolutionising capital raising.

Blockchain technology is a distributed ledger system that records transactions across multiple computers securely, transparently, and tamper-proof. It is the underlying technology behind cryptocurrencies, such as Bitcoin and Ethereum, but it has many other potential applications, including capital raising.

Key features of Blockchain technology

- *Decentralization:* Blockchain networks are decentralised, meaning no single entity controls them. This makes them more secure and resilient to attack.
- *Immutability:* Once data is recorded on a blockchain, it is immutable, meaning it cannot be altered or deleted without the network's consensus. This ensures the integrity and accuracy of the data.
- *Transparency:* Blockchain transactions are transparent and publicly visible. This reduces the risk of fraud and corruption.
- *Security:* Blockchain networks are secured by cryptography, making them very difficult to hack.

How Blockchain can revolutionise capital raising

The global capital raising market is worth trillions of dollars and is snowballing. Traditional capital raising methods are slow, complex, and expensive. Blockchain technology can potentially revolutionise capital raising by addressing these pain points.

The lengthy process is one of the most significant pain points of traditional capital raising. Companies often have to go through multiple capital raising rounds, which can take months or even years to complete. Blockchain can streamline this process by automating many steps, such as due diligence and contract execution. For example, a blockchain-based due diligence platform could be used to verify the identity and credentials of investors and companies. This would eliminate the need for companies to spend months conducting their due diligence.

Another pain point of traditional capital raising is the cost of intermediaries. Companies often pay high fees to investment banks and other intermediaries for their services. Blockchain can eliminate the need for these intermediaries, saving companies money and giving them more control over the capital raising process. For example, decentralised exchanges (DEXs) allow investors to trade assets directly with each other without the need for a central intermediary. This makes it easier for companies to raise capital from investors worldwide. Smart contracts can automate the execution of capital raises. For example, a smart contract could automatically distribute tokens to investors once a specific funding target has been reached. Blockchain can create digital registries for investments and corporate actions. This can make tracking money movement and identifying any suspicious activity easier.

While blockchain can potentially revolutionise capital

raising, some challenges and limitations still need to be addressed. One challenge is the lack of regulatory clarity. Governments around the world are still developing regulations for blockchain technology. This can make it difficult for companies to know how to use blockchain for capital raising in compliance with the law. Another challenge is the complexity of blockchain technology. Blockchain can be difficult to understand and use, especially for businesses unfamiliar with technology.

Despite these challenges, blockchain has the potential to revolutionise capital raising by making it more efficient, transparent, and inclusive.

Blockchain-powered investment vehicles

Blockchain technology has given rise to new and innovative investment vehicles that CEOs can leverage to overcome traditional capital raising hurdles. Some of these investment vehicles include:

- *Security tokens:* Security tokens are digital representations of assets, such as shares in a company, real estate, or commodities. They are issued on a blockchain and can be traded on decentralised exchanges.
- *Initial coin offerings (ICOs)*: ICOs are a way for companies to raise capital by selling tokens to investors. Tokens can give investors access to products or services or be traded for other cryptocurrencies or fiat money.
- *Decentralized autonomous organisations (DAOs):* DAOs are organisations governed by smart contracts on a blockchain. They can be used to raise capital and manage funds transparently and decentralised.

Security Tokens: a game changer

These digital assets represent ownership or a stake in a real-world asset or company. Security tokens are subject to securities regulations and are often used to represent company shares, a fund stake, or ownership of real estate or other assets. They are akin to traditional securities but in a digital or tokenised form.

Security tokens have emerged as a groundbreaking development in capital raising, offering advantages over traditional methods.

Security tokens can be traded on decentralised exchanges, which are more efficient and less expensive than traditional stock exchanges.

Security token transactions are transparent and publicly visible, which reduces the risk of fraud and corruption.
Investors in security tokens typically expect to receive a return on their investment through dividends, profit sharing, or price appreciation of the token. These tokens are often backed by tangible assets or the profitability of the company issuing them.

Their primary purpose is investment. They are designed to represent a stake in an asset and provide the holder with certain rights, such as voting rights or a share in the profits.

Security tokens can be programmed to represent a wide range of assets and to have different rights and privileges. This gives CEOs more flexibility in how they structure their capital raising campaigns.

Initial Coin Offerings (ICOs) and their potential

ICOs have also gained significant attention in recent years, offering CEOs a way to raise capital quickly and efficiently. ICOs represent a shift in funding projects, especially in the technology sector. They demonstrate a move towards more decentralised and democratised forms of investment. It is similar to an IPO. The tokens sold during an ICO can vary in their utility and are not necessarily considered securities.

They allow companies to bypass the rigorous and regulated capital-raising process that venture capitalists or banks require, potentially speeding up the fundraising process significantly.

ICOs can be accessed by a global pool of investors, providing a broader base of potential funding compared to traditional methods. This global reach can be especially advantageous for projects with an international focus or appeal.

In an ICO, investors typically receive digital tokens, which can have various uses within the project's ecosystem, such as granting access to services or acting as a form of currency within the platform. This creates an immediate utility and potential value for the tokens.

ICOs can help build a community of supporters and users around a project. Investors in ICOs are often proponents of the technology or the concept and can become early adopters and brand ambassadors.

While some ICO participants may buy tokens hoping for price appreciation, the primary purpose of these tokens is often utility rather than investment.

ICO tokens often become tradable on various cryptocurrency exchanges, providing liquidity to investors. This can be both a positive aspect of easy exit options for investors and a negative one, as it can encourage speculation.

One of the most significant concerns with ICOs is the lack of regulation, leading to fraud and scams. Investors may face substantial risks due to the unregulated nature of most ICOs. Additionally, the legal status of ICOs and tokens is still being defined in many jurisdictions, which could lead to future regulatory challenges.

Early investors in successful ICOs can realise substantial returns on their investments, sometimes far exceeding traditional investment avenues. However, this potential comes with high risk.

The future of capital raising with Blockchain

The future of blockchain technology in capital raising is poised for significant evolution, driven by advancements in technology and shifts in market dynamics.

Energy-Efficient Consensus Algorithms: One of the major critiques of blockchain technology, particularly those that use proof-of-work (PoW) consensus mechanisms like Bitcoin, is their high energy consumption. In response, there is a growing trend towards more energy-efficient consensus algorithms like proof-of-stake (PoS) and delegated proof-of-stake (DPoS). These algorithms require significantly less computational power and energy, making them more sustainable and cost-effective. This shift could enhance the appeal of blockchain for capital raising by addressing environmental and sustainability concerns.

Integration with Artificial Intelligence (AI): The convergence of blockchain with AI could lead to smarter, more adaptive, and more efficient systems. AI can enhance blockchain's capabilities in predictive analysis, automated decision-making, and data-driven insights. For capital raising, AI can help analyse market trends, assess investment risks, automate complex financial models, and make more data-driven and accurate investment decisions.

Incorporation of the Internet of Things (IoT): Blockchain and IoT integration can create a more interconnected and transparent system for asset management and tracking. In the context of capital raising, IoT devices can provide real-time data on asset performance or utilisation, which can be securely and immutably recorded on a blockchain. This integration can boost investor confidence by providing tangible data on asset performance and usage.

Enhanced Security Protocols: As blockchain becomes more prevalent in capital raising, the need for advanced security protocols grows. Future advancements may include quantum-resistant blockchains, as quantum computing poses a potential risk to current cryptographic methods. Enhanced security measures can increase investor confidence in blockchain-based transactions and systems.

Scalability Solutions: Scalability remains a challenge for many blockchain networks. Solutions like layer 2 protocols, sharding, and sidechains are being developed to address this. Improved scalability can enable the handling of a larger volume of transactions, which is crucial for widespread adoption in capital raising activities.

Regulatory Technology (RegTech): Blockchain can play a significant role in the development of RegTech for automating compliance and reporting. Smart contracts could be programmed to ensure that capital raising activities adhere to relevant regulations automatically, reducing the risk of compliance breaches.

Cross-Chain Interoperability: Future advancements in blockchain technology may include enhanced interoperability between different blockchain networks. This interoperability can facilitate a more seamless transfer of assets and information across various blockchains, broadening the scope and reach of capital raising efforts.

Tokenisation of New Asset Classes: Blockchain could enable the tokenisation of a wider range of assets, including intangible assets like intellectual property, or more complex financial products. This diversification can attract a broader spectrum of investors and open new avenues for capital raising.

Decentralised Finance (DeFi) Innovations: The continuous growth and innovation in DeFi have the potential to introduce new financial instruments and models for raising capital. These might include decentralised lending platforms, liquidity pools, and yield farming, which could offer alternative investment opportunities and funding mechanisms.

Social and Governance Tokens: Beyond pure financial returns, future blockchain advancements may foster the development of social and governance tokens that align with investors' social, ethical, or governance values. This could cater to a growing demographic of socially-conscious investors.

In summary, as blockchain technology continues to mature and integrate with other advanced technologies like AI and IoT, its application in capital raising is likely to become more sophisticated, efficient, and diverse. These advancements promise to expand the possibilities for how companies can raise capital while also addressing current limitations and challenges.

Chapter 23 The Impact of AI

23.1 Impact on Capital Raising

Artificial intelligence (AI) is rapidly transforming the world of finance, and the capital raising process is no exception. AI-powered solutions automate tasks, provide valuable insights, and streamline processes, making it easier for businesses to secure funding.

This chapter explores how AI disrupts and transforms the capital raising process, from investor identification and due diligence to investment decision support and portfolio management. It also discusses the ethical and regulatory considerations associated with AI in finance and provides insights into the future of AI in capital raising.

Investor identification and matchmaking

AI-driven algorithms can analyse vast datasets of investors to identify potential matches with a high degree of precision. This can help businesses to save time and resources in their capital raising efforts and to connect with investors who are most likely to be interested in their investment opportunity. This is already a reality. AI can also be used to personalise investor outreach and engagement strategies. By understanding investor preferences and risk appetites, AI can help businesses tailor their messaging and approach to each investor. This can lead to more effective investor communication and a higher likelihood of success in securing funding.

Investment valuation and risk assessment

AI can be used to develop more accurate and sophisticated investment valuation models. By analysing various financial and non-financial data, AI can identify factors that traditional valuation methods may overlook. This can lead to fairer pricing and more optimised deal structures. AI can also predict potential investment risks based on market trends and company-specific data. This information can be used to develop strategies to mitigate these risks and to make more informed investment decisions.

Due diligence and compliance

AI can automate many tasks involved in due diligence, such as reviewing documents and identifying relevant information. This can significantly streamline the due diligence process, making it faster and more efficient. AI can also automate compliance checks and ensure investments align with relevant regulations. This can reduce legal risks and delays in the capital raising process.

Investor communication and reporting

AI can generate automated reports and updates for investors, providing real-time company performance information. This can help businesses to maintain transparency and build trust with investors. AI-powered chatbots and virtual investor relations officers can also handle investor queries and provide information. This can enhance investor communication and support and free human resources to focus on other tasks.

Crowdfunding and alternative funding

AI is playing a growing role in crowdfunding and alternative funding platforms. AI-powered algorithms can target the right audience for a crowdfunding campaign and fine-tune campaign strategies to maximise success. AI also disrupts traditional lending by automating risk assessment and credit scoring. This makes it easier for small businesses to access capital through peer-to-peer lending and other alternative funding channels.

Predictive analytics will be a game-changer

- *Predicting investor behaviour:* By analysing historical investment patterns and market sentiment, predictive analytics can help identify factors influencing investor decisions, such as economic conditions, industry trends, and regulatory changes. This information can be used to tailor pitch presentations, adjust investment strategies, and anticipate potential investor concerns.

- *Assessing investment opportunities:* Predictive analytics can analyse financial data, market research reports, and competitive intelligence to assess the potential success of investment opportunities. This can help companies identify promising investments with high growth potential and minimise the risk of investing in underperforming or risky ventures.

- *Optimizing capital raising strategies:* Predictive analytics can optimise capital raising strategies by identifying the most effective channels for reaching target investors, maximising the impact of marketing campaigns, and determining the optimal timing for capital raising initiatives.

- *Managing investor expectations:* Predictive analytics can provide insights into investor expectations regarding return on investment, timelines for exits, and potential risks. This can help companies set realistic expectations, manage investor relations effectively, and avoid conflicts or misunderstandings.

- *Identifying potential risks:* Predictive analytics can identify risks associated with investment opportunities, such as legal or regulatory issues, market downturns, or technological disruptions. This information can help companies mitigate risks, protect their investments, and make informed decisions about deal structuring and allocation.

The future of AI in capital raising

AI is rapidly transforming the capital raising process, and this trend will likely continue. Emerging technologies and trends in AI, such as natural language processing and machine learning, are paving the way for new and innovative AI-powered solutions in capital raising.

However, it is essential to note that AI is not a silver bullet. It is important to use AI responsibly and ethically and to be aware of AI systems' potential biases and limitations. Regulators are also working to develop new frameworks to address the ethical and regulatory challenges associated with AI in finance.

Integrating AI into the capital raising process creates new opportunities and efficiencies for entrepreneurs and investors. By understanding AI's potential benefits and challenges, private company CEOs can leverage AI's capabilities and secure funding more effectively.

AI is democratising access to capital by making it easier for businesses of all sizes to connect with investors, regardless of location or network. It enables new forms of capital raising, such as security token offerings (STOs) and initial coin offerings (ICOs). AI is helping to reduce the cost and time associated with capital raising. It makes it possible to raise capital more efficiently and effectively while mitigating risks and protecting investors.

23.2 Impact on Investor Decisions

AI-powered tools and platforms can help investors source deals more efficiently, identify investment opportunities they may have missed, and make better investment decisions.

Sourcing deals

One of the biggest challenges that investors face is sourcing deals. It can take time and effort to identify high-quality investment opportunities. AI-powered tools can help investors automate the deal-sourcing process and identify potential investment opportunities they may have missed.

For example, AI can analyse large datasets of company data to identify companies that are growing rapidly, have strong financials, and are operating in attractive industries. AI can also track social media and news sources to identify companies generating buzz or facing significant challenges.

Identifying investment opportunities

AI can also help investors identify investment opportunities they may have missed. AI-powered tools can analyse data from various sources, including financial statements, market research reports, and news articles, to identify patterns and trends indicating potential investment opportunities. For example, AI can identify companies developing new technologies, expanding into new markets, or acquiring other companies. AI can also identify companies trading at a discount to their intrinsic value.

Making better investment decisions

AI can provide investment recommendations based on a company's financial health, market conditions, and investor goals. This can help investors to make more informed and data-driven investment decisions. Once investors have identified potential investment opportunities, they must decide which investments to pursue. AI can help investors make better investment decisions by giving them insights into different investments' risks and potential rewards. For example, AI can analyse historical data to identify factors that predict investment success. AI can also simulate different investment scenarios and assess each scenario's potential risks and rewards.

Optimising portfolios

AI is also used to optimise investment portfolios by diversifying assets and rebalancing based on changing market conditions. This has the potential to generate higher returns and reduce risks for investors.

Specific examples of AI-powered investment tools and platforms

Several AI-powered investment tools and platforms are available to investors today. Here are a few examples:

- Deal sourcing: Deal sourcing platforms like PitchBook and Crunchbase use AI to help investors identify potential investment opportunities.

- Investment research: Investment research platforms such as FactSet and Sentient use AI to give investors insights into different investments' risks and potential rewards.
- Portfolio management: Tools like Betterment and Wealthfront use AI to help investors build and manage their portfolios.

How AI is changing the way investors work

AI is fundamentally changing the way that investors work. AI-powered tools and platforms are helping investors to source deals more efficiently, identify investment opportunities they may have missed, and make better investment decisions.

As AI becomes more sophisticated and widely adopted, it will likely have an even more significant impact on the investment landscape. In the future, AI may be used to automate many of the tasks currently performed by human investors. This could lead to more efficient and profitable investment markets.

Potential challenges and limitations of AI in investing

While AI has the potential to revolutionise the investment industry, several potential challenges and limitations need to be addressed. One challenge is that AI systems are only as good as the data they are trained on. The AI system can only provide accurate insights or make sound recommendations if the data is complete and accurate. AI systems can be biased. If the AI system is trained on biased data, it will produce biased results. Be aware of this potential bias and take steps to mitigate it. Finally, it is essential to remember that AI systems are not perfect. They can make mistakes, and malicious actors can fool them. Use AI systems responsibly and monitor their performance closely.

AI is a powerful tool that can potentially transform the investment industry. AI-powered tools and platforms can help investors source deals more efficiently, identify investment opportunities they may have missed, and make better investment decisions. As AI becomes more sophisticated and widely adopted, it will likely have an even more significant impact on the investment landscape. However, awareness of AI's potential investment challenges and limitations is crucial.

Chapter 24 Will Robots Take Over

Robotics has infused a fresh wave of innovation in capital raising, particularly in data analysis and risk assessment. We can already see the advantages of using robots in these sectors. However, the question arises: are we on the verge of a robot takeover? I would say not within the next 12 months, but get ready to be awed by the increasing role that robots will play in reshaping the industry.

Robots are the future, but they are not here to replace us. Instead, they can offer a helping hand by automating mundane and repetitive tasks. This allows humans to shift their focus onto more strategic and meaningful objectives, such as building relationships with investors and devising business strategies. Moreover, robots can analyse vast quantities of data in a fraction of the time it takes humans, which can help investors make better-informed decisions and detect fraudulent activities.

As technology evolves, we can expect to see an upsurge in the use of robots in capital raising. However, let's not forget that they are not a substitute for human intellect and foresight but rather an ally to help us achieve greater efficiency and superior decision-making, at least for now.

To illustrate, let me give you some examples of how robots are currently being used in capital raising:

- *Data analysis:* Robots can analyse large amounts of data to identify trends and patterns humans might miss. This can help investors identify promising investment opportunities and assess risk.
- *Risk assessment:* Robots can be used to analyse financial statements and other data to assess the creditworthiness of

potential borrowers. This can help lenders make more informed decisions about who to lend money to.

- *Document preparation:* Robots can be used to generate legal documents, such as offering memoranda and subscription agreements. This can save time and money for lawyers and other professionals involved in the capital raising process.
- *Investor outreach:* Robots can be used to identify and contact potential investors. This can help businesses reach a wider pool of investors and increase their chances of raising capital.
- *Due diligence:* Robots can gather and analyse information about potential investments. This can help investors identify potential risks and make more informed decisions.

Factors that could influence the role of robots in capital raising in the future:

- *Regulatory changes:* Governments may introduce regulations that affect using robots in capital raising. For example, regulations may be needed to ensure that robots are used ethically and that investors are protected from fraud.
- *Investor expectations:* Investors may become more comfortable using robots in capital raising as they become more familiar with the technology and its potential benefits. This could lead to a broader adoption of robots in capital raising.
- *Technological advancements:* As robot technology develops, robots will become more capable of performing complex tasks that require human judgment. This could lead to a greater automation of capital raising activities.

As robot technology continues to develop, we can expect to see even more innovative applications for robots in capital raising. For example, robots could be used to:

- *Negotiate deals*: Robots could be used to negotiate deals between businesses and investors. This could help to speed up the capital raising process and reduce the risk of disputes.
- *Provide investment advice:* Robots could advise individuals and businesses. This could help investors make more informed decisions about where to invest their money.
- *Manage investment portfolios:* Robots could be used to manage investment portfolios. This could help investors save time and money on investment fees.

What will a capital raising robot eventually look like?

Keep your eyes peeled as robot technology continues to evolve and create innovative ideas that create success in raising capital. Let's embrace this exciting future and take capital raising to unprecedented heights! A capital raising robot could take many forms, depending on the specific needs of the organisation or individual using it. Here are a few examples of what a capital raising robot might look like:

- *A chatbot*: One of the most exciting prospects is the chatbot, a computer program that can simulate conversation with human users. A capital raising chatbot could be used to answer questions about a company's capital raising efforts, connect potential investors with the right people to talk to, and even process investments online.
- *A virtual assistant:* Imagine having a virtual assistant driven by a computer program that can understand and respond to natural language commands. A capital raising virtual

assistant could be used to schedule meetings with potential investors, send reminder emails about upcoming capital raising events, and even make phone calls to investors.

- *A humanoid robot:* A humanoid robot is a robot that is designed to look and act like a human. A capital raising humanoid robot could greet potential investors at events and give presentations about the company's business. Could a humanoid robot become part of the executive management team?
- *A software program*: A capital raising software program could be used to manage all aspects of the capital raising efforts, from tracking investor data to analysing capital raising results.

In addition to its physical form, a capital raising robot could also have a variety of other features, such as:

- *Artificial intelligence (AI):* AI could power a capital raising robot's ability to understand natural language, learn from its interactions with potential investors, and make personalised recommendations.
- *Machine learning:* Machine learning could help a capital raising robot identify patterns in data, predict investor behaviour, and optimise capital raising campaigns.
- *Natural language processing (NLP):* NLP could help a capital raising robot understand the nuances of human language, such as sarcasm and humour.
- *Emotion recognition:* Emotion recognition could help a capital raising robot understand the emotional state of potential investors and tailor its interactions accordingly.

Robots can make the capital raising process more efficient, transparent, and data-driven. The timeframe for when the whole capital raising process will be automated and executed by robots is difficult to predict. However, it will likely happen in stages, with different tasks being automated over time. As robot technology continues to develop, we can expect to see even more innovative applications for robots in capital raising.

Author Biography

Rebecca Meijlink was born in the Netherlands and studied International and European Law at Leiden University. Many extracurricular activities and a series of impactful internships, including the ABN AMRO International Traineeship Program in Gibraltar, a traineeship at the United Nations International Labour Organization and Human Rights Commission, and a six-month traineeship in DG I at the European Commission complemented her academic journey.

Rebecca then embarked on a career in finance, initially in project management and operations and then on the trading floor for renowned American banks like JP Morgan, Salomon Brothers, Citigroup, Robertson Stephens, and Bear Stearns, accumulating considerable financial success by her thirties. In 2002, she took a year out and travelled around the world.

In 2003, Rebecca established an award-winning FCA-regulated investment advisory firm. Initially, Rebecca focused on the emerging world of hedge funds, facilitating their capital raising and raising capital from investors globally. Later, coinciding with a move to the Middle East, Rebecca expanded into private equity funds and private companies, concentrating on companies with a strategic angle for the Middle East, providing C-level guidance on capital raising and investor communication.

Back in London, after 15 years abroad including 10 years in the Middle East, Rebecca has authored two books: "In the Fire of Capital" about the Middle East and "Mastering Capital Raising," drawing from her two decades of capital-raising expertise. Rebecca is open to advisory roles to further advise on the learnings in this book.

Printed in Great Britain
by Amazon

36544143R00185